FOREWORD BY JOYCE HUGGETT

EXPLORING CONTEMPLATIVE PRAYER

A PRACTICAL HANDBOOK

GW00646543

PETER DODSON AND MARTIN TUNNICLIFFE

kevin mayhew

Published in 2005 by

KEVIN MAYHEW LTD
Buxhall, Stowmarket, Suffolk, IP14 3BW
E-mail: info@kevinmayhewltd.com
www.kevinmayhew.com

9 8 7 6 5 4 3 2 1 0

ISBN 1 84417 494 8
Catalogue No. 1500861

Cover design by Joseph Attard
Edited by Marian Reid
Typeset by Fiona Connell Finch

Printed and bound in Great Britain

About the authors

Peter Dodson was in Church of England parish ministry from 1961 to 1990. His final appointment was as team vicar in York City Centre where he exercised a particular ministry in spiritual direction and training in contemplative prayer. Prior to ordination, Peter was a professional musician, playing and teaching the French horn. Since 1990, he has been associated with Ripon Cathedral, and has continued teaching music, as well as English, creative writing and contemplative meditation. He still plays the horn, both as amateur and professional, and is also engaged in the composition of orchestral and choral works. He includes reading, walking and gardening among his hobbies.

Martin Tunnicliffe was ordained in the Church of England in 1960 and served as a parish priest in the diocese of Birmingham for 38 years. He joined the Fellowship of Contemplative Prayer (FCP) in 1967 and is currently its Chaplain. He has written numerous articles on contemplative prayer and has also written the official biography of R. G. Coulson, the founder of the FCP (1987, Churchman Publishing). He now lives in retirement in the West Midlands and finds more time to devote to home and family and to pursue other interests including reading, sketching, doing crosswords, and playing the piano.

Contents

		Page
	Foreword by Joyce Huggett	7
	Introduction	11

Part 1 On the way

1	What is Contemplation?	15
2	A Visionary and His Legacy	19
3	Is Contemplation Biblical?	27
4	Help and Encouragement Along the Way	35
5	Becoming Still and Attentive	45
6	Distractions, Positive and Negative	53
7	Get Stuck In!	61

Part 2 Six exercises

	Introduction	75
8	First Exercise: Consider Your Life	77
9	Second Exercise: Your Spiritual Inheritance	83
10	Third Exercise: My Resting Place, My Home, My Desire	89
11	Fourth Exercise: Be Still; Know God	95
12	Fifth Exercise: Your Boundaries	99
13	Sixth Exercise: Resurrection and Life	105

Part 3

	Conclusion	111
	Appendix	113
	Further Reading and Other Resources	115
	Notes	117

Foreword

Way back in the 1970s, while I was on retreat with the Sisters of the Love of God, I spotted a booklet written by Peter Dodson. The subject was contemplative prayer. My pursuit of this method of prayer was in its infancy at the time so, eagerly and gratefully, I devoured the author's insights.

Some ten years later, Peter's publisher invited me to write a commendation for a new book this author had written. Again, the subject was contemplative prayer. Again my prayer life was enriched and my relationship with God deepened as a result of the insights contained within its pages. So much so, that anyone thumbing through my copy of that book today would quickly detect the impact each chapter made on me – so many sentences are underlined and so many paragraphs have a huge star against them so that I can refer to them often. In other words, I am indebted to Peter Dodson for the guidance he has unwittingly given me through his writing.

Imagine, then, how intrigued I was, in the Spring of 2005, to receive a letter inviting me to write a Preface for another book on contemplative prayer written by Peter Dodson and co-author Martin Tunnicliffe. The invitation arrived as I was packing my case in preparation for Spring Harvest where, among other commitments, my mandate was to lead seminars on the same subject as the book: contemplative prayer. To my astonishment and joy some four hundred people attended these seminars each day, underlining the fact that countless Christians in our country today are yearning to experience the richness of this ancient but ever-new method of engaging with God.

The actual manuscript of *Exploring Contemplative Prayer* reached me the day *after* Spring Harvest ended. With the memories of members of my seminar group still fresh in my mind, I started to read Chapter 1, 'What is Contemplation?'. How the members of these seminar groups would have lapped up the short, succinct definitions of contemplation:

> *'Contemplation is the awareness of God known and loved at the core of one's being.'*
> *'Contemplation is the art of paying loving attention to God and his world.'*

How their ears would have pricked up at two other claims that:

> *'Contemplation is listening deeply and attentively to God's Word.'*
> *'Contemplation is biblical.'*

Those attending these seminars would have been helped, too, by the practical suggestions the authors give in response to questions would-be pray-ers often ask:

- *How do I find a place for private prayer?*
- *How can I best cope with distractions?*
- *What is a spiritual director, and how do I find one?*
- *How do I draw up a Rule of Life that is relevant for this stage of my life?*
- *How can I live contemplatively?*

Such was the openness of this group that I believe that, like me, they would have relished the opportunity to meditate on scripture in the way that is described by Martin Tunnicliffe in the second part of *Exploring Contemplative Prayer*. These meditations sound simple and they look undemanding – and, in many ways they are. My own experience as I have made time to engage with them, though, is that they are both simple and profound, life-giving and life-changing – to be used not just once, but to be engaged with over and over again.

In other words, I count it a privilege to recommend this book to anyone who is experiencing within themselves a hunger to pray contemplatively, to those who are seeking an answer to the question: *'What is contemplative prayer?'* and to those whose desire is to delve more deeply into this moving and life-changing method of experiencing the heights and depths and mystery of God's great love. *Exploring Contemplative Prayer* is so much more than a book – it is a companion on the most important journey any of us will ever make – the journey deeper into God.

JOYCE HUGGETT, 2005

Introduction

In a sense, this book has taken over fifty years to write and has several hundred authors. We, Peter Dodson and Martin Tunnicliffe, whose names appear on the cover as 'the authors', both feel that our task has been to put into writing the thinking and praying that has been going on since 1949 within the Fellowship to which we belong. This rather unusual organisation is known as The Fellowship of Contemplative Prayer (FCP). It has no staff, no office, and no subscription. It owes its origin to the dedication of an Anglican priest, Robert G. Coulson (1899–1995). You will be able to read something about this rather remarkable Witness of God's Word in Chapter 2.

The Fellowship, which he founded together with half a dozen like-minded clergymen, is now a loose-knit association of several hundred people of various Christian Churches who feel called, as he did, to try to organise their praying and living on a contemplative basis. The simple rule asks us to set aside some time each day for silent prayer. Most of us also try to meet with others on a regular basis for this purpose, working at it in the way you will find described in this book. So what we, 'the authors', have written is really a compilation of the thoughts and experiences of all those people, and their predecessors, who are and who have been patiently listening at depth to the Word of God over so many years.

More immediately, this book has given us the opportunity to re-present two books on contemplative prayer (now out of print) which Peter wrote in the 1980s, using his experience as a retreat conductor and spiritual director of long standing – *Contemplating the Word* and *Embody the Word* (SPCK, 1987 & 1989). A good deal of the contents of both the older books will be found here, revised and updated.

Also included is some new material by Martin Tunnicliffe which derives from his work as a retreat conductor and as General Secretary then Chaplain of the FCP for over 17 years.

Our styles and approaches are different. We are, nevertheless, speaking with one voice and writing with one intention.* Our hope is that, through this book, God will be glorified; and that you, the reader, will be enabled to enrich your prayer, and to deepen and strengthen your relationship both with those whom Mother Julian called your 'even-cristen' (fellow-Christians), and with the Lord whose truest name is I AM.

PETER DODSON AND
MARTIN TUNNICLIFFE, 2005

* This book has two authors, but you will notice that we freely use the pronoun 'I'. This could refer to either of us, and it doesn't matter which, because each of us is in agreement with the other about what we have written. Our text would be stylistically clumsy if we tried to use the first person plural all the way through.

Part
1

ON THE WAY

1   What is contemplation?

I want to help you to pray and live contemplatively. The first thing I must do is to say what we mean by the word 'contemplation' and the term 'contemplative prayer'. The two certainly overlap, but they are not quite the same thing. Many people have tried to define contemplation. A few examples will yield some initial clues: 'Contemplation is nothing else but the perfection of love'[1] and 'Contemplation is the awareness of God known and loved at the core of one's being'.[2]

A key word here is 'love'. Contemplation is about growing in love. If we take the work of contemplation seriously, we cannot escape the theme of love – of God's inexhaustible love for us, for people everywhere, for the whole of creation. This book should help you towards knowing and loving God more deeply within.

Contemplation has also been called 'the prayer of loving regard' and 'the prayer of loving attention'. That word 'attention' gives another clue. Contemplation is the art of paying rapt and loving attention to God and to his world. Sadly, we live in an age which finds it more and more difficult to pay proper attention to anyone or anything. A solicitor friend once told me that he thought he was good at listening to his clients until he discovered the discipline of contemplative prayer and what attentive listening really means. It transformed his whole approach to those who came to him for help.

Contemplation is about quality of attention, whether it be to art, music or poetry, to people, to the world as a whole and, above all, to God. It has been said that the whole point and purpose of education is to enable us to pay attention.[3] Perhaps that was why my schoolteachers nagged me endlessly to 'Pay attention!' I used to resent it, but not now. Now I realise that paying deep and rapt attention to God and to his world is the whole art of living.

Some years ago I wrote:

> Today's world makes it difficult for God to get his Word in edgeways. Our world is like a great classroom of unruly, noisy and inattentive children. God, like the teacher, is struggling to get through, to make his voice heard in the hope that something will sink in, take root, and bear the kind of fruit that will last. What does the teacher say to such a class? Basically three things: 'Sit up! Shut up! Pay attention!' There we have the three basic requirements for any form of contemplation: sitting straight, being quiet, and paying deep attention to the Word of God.

This gives us further clues. Contemplation involves stillness and silence: 'Contemplation – the word men have used . . . to describe man's struggle to become still enough to reflect the face of God.'[4] Mother Mary Clare, Superior of the Society of the Love of God, has some wise remarks to offer along the same lines.

> The most difficult and most decisive part of prayer is acquiring the ability to listen. To listen, according to the dictionary, is 'attentively to exercise the sense of hearing'. It is not a passive affair, a space when we don't happen to be doing or saying anything and are, therefore, automatically able to listen. It is a conscious, willed action, requiring alertness and vigilance, by which our whole attention is focused and controlled . . . It is the beginning of our entry into a personal relationship with God in which we gradually learn to let go of ourselves and allow the Word of God to speak within us.

Note the phrase 'not a passive affair'. The contemplative way of prayer and life is always a struggle. Struggle and contemplation go hand in hand.[5] Another word is 'wrestle'.

I hope this book will never shy away from facing the joyful/uncomfortable experience of struggling and wrestling, mentally, emotionally and physically, with the discipline and the consequences of giving total attention to the Word of God.

The need for silence and stillness has been emphasised by many writers: 'Whenever the heart is silent the voice of God sounds',[6] 'The first thing necessary in order to hear God is to be quiet, silent',[7] 'In the prayer of stillness we try to hold ourselves open to the impact of the truth of Jesus.'[8] The third of these quotations yields a few more initial clues or insights. In the stillness 'we try to hold ourselves *open*'. Contemplation is about being open and exposed, exposed to the truth, to the truth of God as seen in Jesus. If our contemplation is to be Christian, then silent attention to Jesus, who is *the* Word of God, is crucial. Again, this book will represent an expansion and a justification of this. The word 'open' figures in my own attempts to define what I mean by contemplation. This is one of them:

> Contemplation is a tool by which human beings are encouraged to open themselves to the penetrating Word/Spirit/Life of the Eternal, to rediscover their own Godlike nature, to be set free to live wisely, lovingly and powerfully.

The full meaning of this may become clear later. For the moment, consider contemplation as a tool – as a tool, that is, rather than a toy. Unless you are intending to do a serious job of work, it would be best not to use this particular tool and to put this book away. Contemplation is about putting ourselves into the hands of God, so that he can do something with us: so that he can change and transform the way we are, the way we think, feel and behave. Perhaps God has led you to this book precisely because he has enabled you to see your need for change, for a deeper awareness of him, for a more realistic engagement with the business of daily living. If so, pick up the tool of contemplation gladly and gratefully, but carefully. The point of this book is to show you how to use the tool of contemplation skilfully.

Continuing the definitions, look at the word itself: *contemplation*. It is connected with the word 'temple'. Look up 'temple' in a good dictionary: there we might find it defined as 'an open space in which the gods do their work'. That, perhaps, gives us one of the best clues of all. Christian contemplation is about providing an open space in and through which God may do his searching, probing, healing, transforming, life-giving work. 'Open space' does include a time and place set apart for God. But the open space is really *yourself*. You are the temple. You are the open space, the open mind, heart and will, in and through which God does his wise, loving and powerful work.

Let us draw some of these initial thoughts together. Contemplation is about growing in love, about knowing and loving God perfectly in the depths of our being. It is about giving to God and to his world our total and loving attention. It is about struggling to be still and silent in the presence of God. It is about listening deeply and attentively to the Word of God. It is about being open and exposed to the penetrating power of the Word. It is about being Godlike. It is about being a temple in and through which God may do his work.

The work of contemplation is very simple. You do not have to be well educated or clever to use the tool of contemplation. Contemplation is about loving. As a great contemplative Christian said centuries ago: 'By love he [God] may be caught and held, by thinking never.'[9] If you *are* well educated and even highly intelligent, the contemplative way of prayer and life could be right up your street: as long as you realise that contemplation (refreshingly) is not an intellectual exercise, not a matter of head knowledge but of heart knowledge, the simplicity of knowing and responding to God's loving desire for you. It is a great joy to see someone who is known to be intellectually gifted, transfigured by their discovery that the simplicity of contemplation does not *deny* their intellect but *enhances* it. Contemplation is simple, but it can be enormously far-reaching; and it *is* a struggle.

2

A visionary and his legacy

We now move from the broad picture of contemplation, sketched out in the previous chapter, towards its practical implications – from the 'what?' to the 'how?' of contemplative prayer. This is the main concern of our book. But first, let us look briefly at a portrait of the founder of The Fellowship of Contemplative Prayer, Robert G. Coulson. It was his vision and inspiration which energised many hundreds of ordinary men and women (including the authors of this book) to set out on a voyage of spiritual discovery.

Robert, as he was known to most of the early members of the Fellowship, was born in St Petersburg of an English father and a Balt mother.[1] The family had built up a fortune with a large and successful textile business in Estonia manufacturing, among other things, uniforms for the army of the Czar. One of Robert's early memories was of Czar Nicholas II visiting their home and factories. The family were substantial landowners, and Robert would have inherited a very large fortune, if it had not all been confiscated at the time of the Russian revolution in 1917. Later, Robert said that the loss of this inheritance was the best thing that could have happened to him.

Robert would never have described himself either as a visionary or a mystic, but both those words apply when we look at the way his spirituality developed during and after the Second World War. Up until then religion, in any deeply spiritual sense, played no part in his life. In his experience, religion was confined within the strait-jacket of public school and military convention, compulsory chapel and church parades.

His life, however, was by no means without colour and incident. The family barely escaped with their lives from the onslaught of the Bolshevik revolution in 1917. They then settled in England in modest circumstances very different from the grandeur of Estonian high society. After his education at private school and Sandhurst Military Academy, Robert became an army officer. He fought with the White Russians against the Bolsheviks in North Russia, and later served in Germany during the 1920s. Being fluent in French and German, as well as Russian, meant that he had a good deal to offer as a liaison officer with the army of occupation in the Rhine valley.

Robert left the Army in 1929 and, during the 1930s, he was engaged in voluntary social work among the un-employed in London. During this time he began to study, and to read deeply in history, philosophy and psychology. He toyed with the idea of becoming a writer and had three books published of a more or less documentary nature, drawing on his Russian childhood as well as his military and social work background.

During this period, religion meant little to him beyond keeping up appearances. 'Occasionally I attended a service, partly to remain on civil terms with the vicar of the village I lived in, who was my nearest neighbour, and partly to set an example to the villagers, although what that example was intended to exemplify I hardly knew.' Yet all the while, Robert was carrying within him the memory of two remarkable incidents in his life, which made him think that God had perhaps marked him out for a spiritual journey that was to be undertaken when the time was right.

The first of these was a mystical experience which he had had in Estonia when he was about 13 or 14 years old. This is the account from the biography *Spirit and Life*:[2]

I can only say that for moments – minutes perhaps – one felt as though the universe had come down about one's ears like a swarm of bees; you know, the stars buzzing about one's ears, or that one was raised up into the universe, and I look back on it as an extraordinary foretaste of what I tried to get at in my book, you know; that we've got to expand our consciousness, like a tremendous expansion of self-hood and wholeness. It didn't frighten me, but it was so enormous that I thought 'Well, you must have the stomach-ache or something like that; you must have eaten something odd.'

I just pushed it behind me; it was only gradually I realised that was when the Lord said 'Now, look here, you get on your toes, or I'll have to give you a push one day', and it turned out to be like that.

That was how he described it in a recorded interview. He wrote about it more formally in his notes, using the third person:

During this period he had a 'mystical experience' entirely out of the blue, which much later with hind-sight he could best describe as a few minutes of trans-cendentally enhanced selfhood. This enhancement was so ineffably vast that he failed to take the whole experience seriously enough to remember it as more than an incomprehensible chance fact, until many years later.

The second, perhaps even more shattering, event occurred in the forests of North Russia when, as a young subaltern, Robert was part of the British force sent to assist in the (as it turned out) fruitless struggle against the Bolsheviks.

The enemy were the more numerous, but the allies were better disciplined and usually came out quite well in the skirmishes which ensued in and out of the forest and through the peasant villages. There were reversals, however, and it was on one such occasion that Robert's second 'miracle' occurred. His patrol was ambushed in dense forest at 3 o'clock one morning (it was, of course, nearly light, being the arctic summer). The men panicked, for all that they were, as Robert puts it, 'seasoned old sweats – and at the very moment when my platoon sergeant was pressing his trigger, I stepped three yards in front of him'. Robert was quite literally shot in the back of the head. He should, of course, have been killed outright, but instead he was knocked unconscious and left for dead. Fortunately, he regained consciousness a few seconds later and just caught a glimpse of one of his men disappearing in rapid retreat through the trees. He struggled to his feet and managed to stagger after him leaving the Bolsheviks just forty yards away in the other direction, too astonished to shoot with any accuracy. When he went for medical treatment it was discovered that what they thought had been a lucky graze on the back of the head turned out to have been a direct hit – from a dud round!

The official statistics indicated that about one round in 200,000 was faulty. What he thought of then as a phenomenal piece of luck, Robert later interpreted with hindsight as the directing hand of God giving a clear indication that he had a task for him to fulfil in this life which was not to be frustrated by any premature attempts on the part of fickle fortune to end it.

When hostilities began again in 1939, Robert enlisted once more for military service. It was then that the guiding hand of God began to direct him more firmly along the spiritual path that was to become his life's work. At the time, this Divine guidance appeared to be no more than a series of chance meetings with various key philosophers, scientists and theologians in London. These people were in part concerned with religion in the armed forces, but were more acutely aware, under the direction of the Archbishop of Canterbury, Dr William Temple, of the need for a radical spiritual renewal within the British Church and society once the war was over, when the country would be trying to rebuild itself in the post-war situation.

In this stimulating and thought-provoking company, Robert began to study the Scriptures, seeing them in a new light. At the same time, tutored by a Hindu swami, he learnt to meditate, often meeting in cellars during the

London Blitz. In a very short time, he started to see with great clarity how the Word of God and the practice of deep reflective prayer could fuse together with the intellect and create a powerful and purposeful stimulus for spiritual growth. God, instead of being little more than a remote possibility behind the universe, suddenly became for Robert a living reality. It seemed right, therefore, when the war ended, for him to accept the suggestion of the Bishop of Rochester to offer himself for ordination to the sacred ministry within the Church of England.

Robert was to complete fifteen years of parish ministry in Kent. What impression did he give at this time to his parishioners? It was hardly that of a stereotypical vicar. At the age of forty-six, married and with two daughters, he was tall, of military bearing as we might expect, good-looking though without being conventionally handsome, well-dressed to the point of elegance and had charming upper-class manners. At the same time he was quite rigorous in self-discipline, almost frighteningly intelligent, and authoritative.

What was more important, he was clearly fired with enthusiasm and longing to teach and to share with others the vision of the living reality of God that had come upon him during the wartime years. It seemed essential that Christians should experience at first hand and in depth this living spiritual reality by learning how to pray contemplatively. So Robert used every opportunity he could to try to persuade both his flock and his fellow-clergy of the need for spiritual renewal by way of a deepening of their prayer life.

His efforts were not crowned with great success at first. The majority of his parishioners, and probably also of his fellow-clergy in the diocese of Rochester, were still cast in the mould of that conventional church religion that had cut so little ice with Robert himself before the war. But eventually, by means of lectures, short retreats, prayer groups, and also by his writings which began to circulate to a wider and more receptive audience, he was able, in 1949, to found a fellowship for contemplative prayer. It consisted of six clergymen who agreed to subscribe to a simple Rule of Life and to meet annually for a retreat. The method of prayer was, from the start, based on contemplative listening to the Word of God, similar to the method described in this book.

Ten years later, there were thirty-eight members of the Fellowship, all clergy. Then, during the 1960s, the Fellowship was opened up to lay people and the membership began to be numbered in the hundreds. From 1960 onwards, Robert was able to retire from parochial duties and he devoted the rest of his long life, until his death in 1995, to the Fellowship which he regarded as his 'second family'. In addition to hours spent each day in contemplation and intercession, he wrote four books concerned with the theory and practice of contemplative prayer. He also maintained as close a personal contact as he could with the membership. He was a conscientious and prolific correspondent, much sought-after for his spiritual wisdom and guidance.

At the time of the publication of this book, the legacy of Robert G. Coulson is to be seen in the 500 or so signed up members of the Fellowship of Contemplative Prayer in Britain, the 70 to 80 members in Ireland and an equal number in South Africa, together with other members in the US and Australia. Many of these people meet regularly in groups for silent prayer. Non-members often also regularly attend the groups. Consequently, in addition to the membership, there is an unknown number of people who share in the founder's vision and legacy.

Further details of the FCP can be found in the Appendix at the end of this book, but we will allow Robert himself to have the last word in this chapter. As an ex-soldier, he was fond of using military analogies. Here is a lively illustration about hearing and doing the Word of God which he wrote in one of his letters:

I had been contemplating the saying from Ezekiel 12, Verse 28: 'No Word of MINE shall be delayed; even as I speak it shall be done.' I suddenly remembered the experience at Sandhurst, aged 17, of being drilled by our Adjutant in 1917 or 1918. He was a Scots Guards Major who was unfit for active service owing to severe wounds [sustained] earlier in the war. He was left with one eye, and was said to be all tied up with wire inside. He exercised iron discipline, but always gently, almost politely. He drilled us 1100 cadets without apparently much raising his voice, and with his one eye spotted our slightest mistake. A really wonderful man.

One can imagine what 1100 youths of 17–18 years of age could be [like]. However, we practically worshipped him. He could do anything with us. Now, *sometimes* the experience of being drilled by him rose to an almost mystical degree, especially at a ceremonial parade. I suddenly felt at one with the 1100 of us, all intent on instantly obeying the word of command. We would have faced any danger in doing so. It is better to say no more to avoid the risk of bathos.

This memory of seventy years ago has helped me to *begin* to understand what I AM means by saying: 'No word of MINE shall be delayed . . .' Also the other things he says about his Words.'[3]

3 Is contemplation biblical?

I have emphasised that contemplation is to do with giving rapt and loving attention to the Word of God. The Bible is sometimes called the Word of God. This expresses rather loosely a truth about the Bible. It is far better to consider the Bible as the *primary source* of God's Word. The Bible on my desk is scruffy and dog-eared. Its back is broken. You may have come across a delightful poster that proclaims, 'Bibles that are falling apart are usually read by people who aren't.' It might be better to say that Bibles that are falling apart are usually read and *prayed* by people who aren't.

The Bible gives us a two-sided vision: a vision of God, and a vision of what it means to be the people of God. The Old Testament gives us a growing insight into that two-sided vision. Men like Moses, Isaiah, Jeremiah and Hosea struggle to see God and to see what it means to be his people: what it means to be truly human.

In the New Testament we are presented with Jesus Christ. In him we see the two sides of that vision wrapped up together. In him we see the vision of God *and* what it means to be people of God. In Jesus we see true humanity: humanity at its very best, humanity to perfection. This is what we mean by the incarnation: God and humanity wrapped up together. Jesus, say both the Bible and the contemplative, *is* the Word of God. He is the incarnation, the embodiment of the Word. He is the Word of God in the flesh:

> In the beginning was the Word, and the Word was with God, and the Word was God. He was in the beginning with God; all things were made through him, and without him was not anything made that was made. In him was life, and the life was the light of men. The Light shines in the darkness, and the darkness has not overcome it . . . And the Word was made flesh and dwelt among us.
>
> John 1:1–5,14, RSV

Words like 'vision' and 'image' are closely connected. In the vision of Jesus may be seen the perfect image (icon) of God (Hebrews 1:1–3). In him may be seen the power and wisdom and love of the mind and heart and will of God – God's radiant glory.

Our own humanity is marred. The image of God in us is badly distorted. Contemplation is about having vision: a vision of God and of humanity at its best. Contemplation is about the 'restoration of the divine image in human nature'.[1] Jesus is crucial, not only to our own vision and restoration, but to the vision and restoration of all humanity and of all creation.

St Paul put it this way: 'We, who with unveiled faces all reflect the Lord's glory, are being transformed into his likeness with ever increasing glory' (2 Corinthians 3:18, NIV). By contemplating *him* we become like him.

So, is contemplation biblical . . . according to the Scriptures? Let us begin to answer this with a further set of questions and then turn to the Bible for the answer. Does God *want* his people to be still and silent and to listen to him? Does he *want* to penetrate us with his Word or words? Does he *want* his Word or words to live in us so that they motivate all that we are and all that we do? What follows is a selection of texts from the Bible using various authorised translations. They demonstrate that the answer to our questions is a resounding 'Yes!' (The biblical references are given in the endnotes.)

Old Testament

The Lord our God says to his people: 'Listen! Listen to ME. Listen MY people. Be silent before ME. Be still. Be attentive to every word of MINE. It is to you I call, MY people who know what is right, you who lay MY law to heart. Draw near to ME. Listen carefully to all that I have to say to you, and take it to heart.

'I will speak clearly, you will have plain speech from ME. I speak nothing but truth. All that I say is right, all is straightforward. I declare what is just.

'Listen to ME and grow wise. Listen to ME and you will have good food. Hold fast to my words with all your heart, keep my commandments, and you will have life. The person I look to is one who reveres MY words. I put MY words in your mouth. Are not my words like fire; are they not like a hammer that shatters rock? You must listen to what I say. You must speak MY words. I will give you the power of speech.

'I, the Lord, will say what I will, and it shall be done; I will speak, I will act. No words of MINE shall be delayed; even as I speak, it shall be done. Go, tell everything, declare and proclaim among the nations, spread the news, keep nothing back. MY words which I put into your mouth will never fail you. As the rain and the snow come down from heaven and do not return until they have watered the earth, so shall the word which comes forth from MY mouth prevail; it shall not return to ME fruitless, without accomplishing MY purpose.'

In these texts, we are at the very heart of the prophetic ministry: exposure to the Word, the indwelling of the Word, and the proclamation of the Word.

The Gospel

Our Lord Jesus Christ says to his people: 'Listen to ME and understand. To you who are MY friends I say, "Do not fear. Be still, be silent, be opened. Take note of what you hear."

What I say is for you. Take care how you listen. MY task is to bear witness to the truth, and all who are not deaf to truth listen to MY voice. Anyone who loves ME will heed what I say. The words I speak to you are both spirit and life. MY words will never pass away.

'What I say to you, I say to everyone. What I say to you, you must repeat. What you hear, you must shout from the housetops. Go and tell everything God has done for you. You must go and announce the kingdom of God. Go and proclaim the Good News to the whole creation. The words you need will be given you. I MYSELF will give you power of utterance. Say whatever is given you to say; for it is not you who will be speaking, but the Holy Spirit.'

There are striking similarities in these two collections of words from the Lord. Even though they are only a mere handful of the Bible's countless words, they represent the very heart of scripture. This is precisely the traditional claim of the contemplative life: that it represents the very essence of scripture. The contemplative life takes seriously the command to 'Be silent before the Lord' (Zephaniah 1:7, RSV), to 'Be attentive to every word of MINE' (Exodus 23:13, REB) so that every word will 'accomplish MY purpose' (Isaiah 55:11, REB).

Did *Jesus* pray in this way? Again the answer is a clear 'Yes!' 'A great while before day, he rose and went out to a lonely place, and there he prayed' (Mark 1:35, RSV). He 'went out into the hills to pray; and he spent the whole night in prayer' (Luke 6:12, JB). St Luke tells us that 'he would always go off to some place where he could be alone to pray' (Luke 5:16, JB).

This is a contemplative attitude. Contemplation is total absorption in prayer. Contemplation is 'loving God and letting him love us'.[3] Jesus spent much time giving loving attention to God and letting God love him. It was the kind of experience that enabled him to say things like 'As the Father has loved me, so I have loved you' (John 15:9, RSV). Contemplation is about loving God and loving people.

Jesus was also, like the true contemplative, a living witness to the spirit of the Psalms, especially those that speak of stillness, waiting, and the desire to know God: 'As a deer longs for a stream of cool water, so I long for you, O God. I thirst for you, the living God', 'Be still then, and know that I AM God', 'I wait patiently for God to save me', 'O God, you are my God, and I long for you. My whole being desires you; my soul is thirsty for you', 'O God, my heart is ready, my heart is ready'.[4]

If you do not already know the 'Sayings' in the last paragraph by heart, it would be a good idea to learn them now, using them as a sound preparation for the challenging work of hearing, receiving and living by the Word of God.

Reference has already been made to the penetrating, searching, probing power of the Word. In the Old Testament, God is represented as saying, 'I, the Lord, search the mind and test the heart' (Jeremiah 17:10, NEB). In the New Testament, the Word of God is said to be 'alive and active: it cuts like any double-edged sword, but more finely: it can slip through the place where the soul is divided from the spirit, or joints from the marrow; it can judge the secret emotions and thoughts. No created thing can hide from him; everything lies uncovered and open to the eyes of the one to whom we must give account of ourselves' (Hebrews 4:12–13, JB).

The sword is a vital image of the Word. St Paul speaks of the 'sword of the Spirit which is the word of God' (Ephesians 6:17, RSV). In the Revelation to John, we are presented with a vision of the exalted Christ and 'out of his mouth came a sharp sword, double-edged' (Revelation 1:16, JB).

We might think instead of a surgeon's scalpel which cuts 'more finely'. The contemplative experience is that the Word of God has a fine cutting edge, sharp and fine as a scalpel. It is the cutting edge of truth, spoken in love. The Word has the power to get right under the skin – to probe our innermost thoughts and desires. It is a kind of gentle open-heart surgery. There is no anaesthetic; only the love of God and his patient ability to probe to the heart. There can be pain, sometimes almost overwhelming pain, but *never* more than we can cope with.

The contemplative way of prayer allows God to use the sword of his Spirit. The contemplative discipline can also arm us with the same sword as an effective spiritual weapon when it comes to dealing with *the alternative voice*. This is the voice of temptation, traditionally ascribed to the tempter, the devil. We are all susceptible to this alternative voice which will suggest that we follow this or that course of action that we know to be contrary to the will of God. At such times it is important to grasp the 'sword of the spirit which is the Word of God', and focus attention on some particular saying such as, 'Do not be afraid, for I AM with you' (Isaiah 41:10, JB).

When Jesus went through his desert experience, he was plagued by that alternative voice.[5] But he was supremely armed with the Word and Spirit of God. The tempting voice of the devil would say one thing; Jesus would retort that God had something different to say. Of particular significance to contemplatives is Jesus' desert proclamation that 'Man . . . live(s) by every word that proceeds from the mouth of God' (Matthew 4:4, RSV). The contemplative way is about living by the Word.

The sword is one valuable image. Another is 'seed'. When Jesus explained the Parable of the Sower, he said 'The seed is the word of God . . . The seeds that fell in good soil stand for those who hear the message and retain it in a good and obedient heart, and they persist until they bear fruit' (Luke 8:11,15, GNB).[6]

The best possible soil in which God may sow the seed of his Word is the soil of silence and stillness. Any gardener will know that when you move the soil about, seeds cannot get rooted, which is why we keep busy with the hoe to keep the weeds down. Seeds can only grow when the soil is still.

It is the same with human beings. When we can learn to be still – to be still not just with our bodies but with our minds and hearts – the 'Word-seed' can find a place to rest, to germinate, put down strong roots, grow, flourish and bear abundant fruit. The contemplative way is about persisting with the discipline, not only of hearing the Word, but of keeping it in the heart and allowing it to grow and become fruitful – fruitful for the service of God and his world. Church of England prayer books have consistently maintained that it is part of our Christian duty to hear *and receive* God's holy Word.

In addition to good soil, seeds need warmth. The Scriptures also refer to God's nature and Word in terms of heat and fire. 'Our God is a consuming fire,' says the writer of the letter to the Hebrews (12:28, RSV, quoting Deuteronomy 4:24). The Lord says to the prophet, 'I will make my words a fire in your mouth' (Jeremiah 5:14, REB). The fire of God's love also has a cleansing and purifying effect, the power to purge away all that is bad in us, leaving us as good as precious metal which has been 'tried in the fire' (Zechariah 13:9, Malachi 3:1–3).

This purging process may, of course, take a lifetime and more than a lifetime, but the discipline of contemplation does enable us to be exposed to the cleansing process of the Word of God (John 15:3). As we begin to know this Word of love alive and active within us, we can also begin to make Jeremiah's words our own: 'His word is in my heart like a burning fire, shut up in my bones. I am weary of holding it in; indeed, I cannot' (Jeremiah 20:9, NIV). Such a person is fuelled and fired for mission.

The Bible contains more than forty different images of the Word. Each one is capable of exciting the imagination and enhancing our appreciation of the Word. We have looked briefly at three of them: the sword, the seed and the fire. We shall be touching on some of the others.[7] But the point has been made that both the Old and New Testaments of the Bible are a *primary* source of the Word.

4 Help and encouragement along the way

So far, we have looked at something of the *meaning* of contemplation, at *motives* for doing it, and at its *biblical* basis. If this has made sense, we can now begin to look at some practical matters which will be of help as you set out along this particular path in prayer.

In one way or another we have tried to make it clear that contemplative prayer, though simple, is far from easy. Unless you are a really exceptional person such as one of those very few people who are called by God to the solitary life of prayer, the true hermit, you will not be able to undertake the work of contemplative prayer without the support and encouragement of others. So it is both sensible and of great benefit to belong to a wider fellowship of people who feel themselves drawn to a contemplative way of life. I am assuming that you are not called to be a monk or a nun. Nevertheless, it is still possible for ordinary lay people to have a strong personal link with a monastic community. Two that come to mind, for men and women respectively, are the Community of the Servants of the Will of God and the Sisters of the Love of God (see Appendix). Such religious communities offer associate membership of various kinds, produce valuable pamphlets and other occasional literature, and normally appoint one of their number to keep a personal eye on each associate member.

There are other, *non*-monastic fellowships dedicated to the encouragement of silent prayer, such as our own Fellowship of Contemplative Prayer, which offer a similar kind of support and help (see the Appendix for details).

If you are really serious about exploring the deeper levels of prayer, it is often a good idea to be associated with such a community or fellowship. A link of this kind will be tremendously valuable and significant, as you grow in the spirit.

Finding a spiritual director

The contemplative way is like a journey – a journey in the course of which we encounter both pleasant and unpleasant things. There are joyful moments and painful moments. You will most likely encounter obstacles and setbacks along the way. Sometimes you may find yourself in total darkness, afraid, not knowing where you are or which direction to take.

Belonging to a supportive group, such as those we have just mentioned, can obviously be extremely helpful as you undertake this voyage. So too, could membership of your local church act as a kind of beacon or lighthouse to help you gain or regain a sense of purpose and direction. In addition, many people find it helpful, and some believe it to be essential, to have a spiritual guide or director, a wise and understanding 'soul friend' to travel alongside them on their contemplative journey. That friend's job is simply to love you, to be with you in your moments of darkness and fear, to keep you safe, and to help you grow in confidence along the way.

If you are an associate member of a monastic community, that 'soul friend' may be the person into whose care you have been placed. Alternatively, your spiritual guide could be your parish priest or minister, or the leader of a local contemplative prayer group. Whoever you choose, it is important that they themselves should be exploring a contemplative way, have a spiritual director of their own, be able to relate to you easily, to talk the kind of language you understand, and to be the kind of person you feel able to trust. The real value of a spiritual director is that, with your permission and co-operation, he or she can get to

know you well, perhaps even better than you know yourself. One of the snares along the spiritual path is self-
deception, and a good director can help you to avoid that
pitfall.

Assume, then, that you see the good sense in having a
spiritual director or guide, that you decide to put yourself
into someone's hands. From the very beginning, both you
and your director must understand that, initially at least,
the arrangement is for a trial period. If, at any point, it
becomes clear that the director is not the right person for
you, then you must both have total freedom to part
company – freedom that gives you the opportunity to find
a different person to guide you. Sensitive directors will
understand this and will often suggest another person who
may be suitable.

For those who have been brought up in the Catholic
tradition, your director may also be your confessor. This is
not essential but it can be a good arrangement. Either way,
it is obvious that sinfulness must put obstacles in the path
of those who tread the contemplative way, and the
discipline of sacramental confession (now often called the
ministry of reconciliation) can be a strong support and
may be essential if the way seems completely and unaccountably blocked.

Adopting a Rule of Life

The monastic community or prayer fellowship with which
you may be associated, as well as your director or confessor, will almost inevitably encourage you to consider
adopting a 'Rule of Life'. This Rule is usually tailor-made
to fit your own circumstances. Such a Rule need not be
harsh or rigid, but is more likely to be compassionate and
gentle, taking into consideration our limitations of time,
energy, character and ability. The point of the Rule is to
enable us to achieve at least some sense of *order* in our
lives, some creative use of our time, talents and poss-
essions. Like contemplation itself, the Rule is a valuable

tool, enabling us to be disciplined about the things that really matter.

It may be that you have not so far come across a Rule of Life. Here for your consideration is the Rule adopted by our Fellowship of Contemplative Prayer. It is a corporate Rule as much as a personal one, helping Fellowship members to feel that they are sharing and supporting one another in it. It is accepted for one year at a time:

I undertake for one year from now to commit myself as far as I am able:

- to set aside at least one period daily in order to become still, and in contemplation to receive the words of God (spoken to us through Christ) and thereby the inspiration of the Holy Spirit, as deeply as I can;
- to remember before God in prayer at least once a week, if possible on a Wednesday, the Fellowship in general, and those members individually whom I know personally.

A note is added that the Rule implies that members will make use of Sayings from the Bible for the purpose of silent contemplative prayer according to the method and pattern which the Fellowship has learnt from the teaching and example of its founder Robert Coulson. The Rule is basic and simple, and the key words 'as far as I am able' should be noted. Any Rule, whatever form it may take, will almost inevitably be broken. We tend to be such distracted, undisciplined creatures. Those who are accustomed to making their confession will know only too well how the confessor will hear time and again, the same failures repeated. So another note appended to the Fellowship Rule reads: 'It has been found that a simple Rule which *all* members *try* to keep is far more effective than a more elaborate one that only some fitfully practise. Yet no one who tries should ever feel guilty in the case of occasional failure to keep it; the only real failure is to stop trying.'

This Rule, like any Rule worthy of the name, is a call to holiness. Contemplation is about responding to God's command to 'Be holy, for I, the Lord your God, am holy' (Leviticus 20:7). So the Rule does give us a standard to aim for, a practical structure within which to struggle to live the contemplative way.

Exploring the Bible

We have looked at some of the tools of the job. We have seen something of the value of a wider fellowship, a spiritual director and a Rule of Life. In Chapter 3 we began to see the value of the Bible as a tool for contemplative prayer.

We have already stated that contemplation is not an intellectual exercise. But one of the *effects* of contemplation is a growing, even a compelling desire to explore the Scriptures, including biblical theology. Contemplative prayer will almost certainly instil within us a hunger to get to grips with the great biblical themes and to plumb the depths of the key words of the Hebrew/Christian Scriptures. Some kind of disciplined Bible reading and Bible study becomes essential. Your local church and its worship should provide a focus for this.

Today we are fortunate that, whether you are engaged in Bible reading and study on your own or with other people, there are numerous aids available to help you out. There are many excellent modern translations, and it is always useful to read texts in more than one version. For contemplative purposes, don't reject the traditional Authorised (1611) and Revised (1884) Versions which are often more devotional than modern versions and can sometimes convey a deeper understanding of the spiritual sense which lies beneath the surface meaning. You should look for other helpful literature on your church bookstall and in the religious bookshops, and it is always good to ask for guidance from your minister and spiritual director. A small selection of currently useful literature may be found in the Appendix and endnotes.

For the contemplative, the Bible can come alive; it can stimulate and excite. The contemplative use of scripture can enable us to cut through a good deal of its 'cultural clutter' and to grasp its essential message. Because we are *praying* the Bible as well as reading and studying it – because we are in touch with the *spirit* of scripture – God is able to speak to the heart directly, plainly and incisively.

Living the contemplative life

Following the contemplative way can instil a strong awareness of one's own worth and value. Again, this may happen suddenly, even traumatically, or it may dawn gently and slowly. The effect is to make us less and less inclined to do things that are self-destructive, and to wish to do things that enhance rather than diminish our humanity. Contemplative prayer is about embodying the love of God and being a channel of that love for other people and for the world. To do this vital work we need to be as fit as possible: not just mentally and emotionally fit, but also physically fit.

There is a story of a young man who came to that great bishop of the Orthodox Church, Metropolitan Anthony Bloom, to talk about spirituality and prayer. After some intellectual and, to the bishop's mind, somewhat ineffectual conversation on the topic, the bishop said to the young man, 'I want you to go away, and do a five-mile run before breakfast every morning for six weeks. Then you can come back and talk about prayer.'

Note that we talk about being 'as fit as possible'. You may, perhaps, have some physical limitation or disability, something over which neither you nor your doctor can exercise effective control – something you just have to live with. Or you may, or course, simply be advanced in years. All that is required is that we take responsibility for being as fit as we *can* be: that we give our bodies a reasonable amount of exercise; that we are careful not to spend an excessive amount of time slouched lazily, for instance, in front of the television set; that we do not work ourselves to the point of exhaustion so that we are fit for nothing and no one; that we give ourselves time for adequate sleep and relaxation; that we are careful about what we eat and drink.

A word about fasting is appropriate here. Being careful about diet is not the same as fasting. A fast means a time of going without solid food. This may be for a day, a weekend, a week, or even longer. As a religious act, fasting is itself a form of prayer.

> It is a praying with the body, affirming the wholeness of the person in spiritual action; it gives emphasis and intensity to prayer; specifically it expresses hunger for God and his will . . . it is a training in Christian discipline and specifically against the sin of gluttony; it expresses penitence for the rejection and crucifixion of Christ by the human race; it is a following of Jesus on his way of fasting . . . [1]

If you are called to the discipline of fasting, then this must be done carefully and responsibly. It may be necessary to consult your doctor to see if you are physically fit enough to take on the rigour of a fast. In any case, if you do feel drawn to this discipline, you should at least read a good book on the subject, not necessarily a religious one.[2]

The practice of contemplation should also lead to a decreasing need for self-destructive stimulants such as alcohol, tobacco, drugs and unhealthy sex. The experience of contemplation and the disciplines related to it can be in themselves stimulating, invigorating, refreshing, bracing, energising, rejuvenating. Basically, the leading of a truly disciplined prayer life encourages us to let go of destructive stimulants simply because we know ourselves to be made in the image of God, know that we are profoundly loved and valued by him and that we are to live and work for his praise and glory.

A culture of silence

We are concerned in this book with the prayer of silence and stillness. It is a temptation to use this kind of prayer as an escape mechanism, a means whereby we can ourselves be mentally and physically refreshed, so that we can then return to our customary world of bustle, noise and chatter. You should, however, ask yourself from time to time to what extent you are yourself responsible for the climate of noise and unrest which you habitually inhabit.

There is no doubt that, if we are to *hear* and *receive* (and ultimately *do*) God's holy Word, then we need to allow a personal culture of silence to grow around and within us during the course of our daily lives. In our contemporary world, this is to swim against a veritable tidal wave of noise and almost ceaseless clatter and chatter. How many of your friends and acquaintances are compulsive talkers? And when you come to analyse it, how much of the talk is really useful, instructive, necessary, or even interesting or entertaining? How many of them reach for the radio or TV switch, especially at that most precious time in the early morning, when a recollected mind, even in the midst of early morning chores, can set the tone for the day ahead? Patrick Woodhouse has written an interesting book called *Beyond Words*.[3] This is some of what he has to say about silence:

> We need silence. Silence in the Christian tradition is far more than the absence of noise. It has been called 'the first language of God'. Silence more than anything else takes us into the Mystery itself. So although times of prayer may include words and music, it is above all an adventure in silence. However, like being alone, being silent also goes against the grain, and may be something that is quite hard to keep to in many households. From the moment we wake in the morning and turn on the radio, to the last moment of the day when the TV is turned off we surround ourselves with incessant noise. There is a need to fill the blank and even

threatening emptiness that silence would suggest. So there can be a deep resistance to silence and at first we do have to 'force ourselves' into it. However, if we stay with it we find that it brings huge rewards – sometimes what feels like a kind of breakthrough to another dimension of being.

To nurture a personal culture of silence will be easier for some people than for others. To some extent it depends on the environment in which we live. For some it comes naturally. You occasionally come across people who, however turbulent their home or work setting, seem to be able to retain a personal peace and tranquillity. For most of us, however, it is a matter of self-discipline, sometimes applied quite strictly. This is not simply our observance of a daily quiet time, but a conscious decision to live day by day without constant recourse to the clamour of the media or to pointless talking. To fill one's life with noise and chatter is often merely a habit which, like other habits, can become addictive. But the deliberate *avoidance* of unnecessary talk and clamour can also become habitual, and when it does, we begin to value more and more those God-given moments of tranquillity and peace when they arrive. If you cultivate the habit of stillness, you will find that, when the time comes for contemplative prayer, not only will you slip into it more easily, but you will have fewer distractions and your prayer-time will become far more purposeful.

All of what I have tried to say is borne out by the classical writers and teachers in the great tradition of spirituality and authentic mysticism. Here are just two characteristic quotations: the first from the fourth century and the second from the twentieth century:

> Many are avidly seeking, but they alone find who remain in continual silence. Every man who delights in a multitude of words, even though he says admirable things, is empty within. If you love truth, be a lover of silence. Silence like the sunlight will illuminate you in God and will deliver you from the

phantoms of ignorance. Silence will unite you to God himself. More than all things love silence; it brings you a fruit that tongue cannot describe. In the beginning we have to force ourselves to be silent. But then there is born something that draws us to silence. May God give you an experience of this 'something' that is born of silence. If only you practise this, untold light will dawn on you in consequence . . . after a while a certain sweetness is born in the heart of this exercise and the body is drawn almost by force to remain in silence. *Isaac of Nineveh*

The darkness of silence has to be penetrated before its final sequence, the passage of the soul to God, is traversed. The first use of silence is to explore the depths of our own personality, to come to terms with the fears and inhibitions that lie deeply placed in the unconscious part of the mind. The second use of silence is to be able to listen to what other people are actually saying to us. When we are silent within we can, perhaps for the first time, begin to perceive the message of another person and listen to him with attention and concern. The third use of silence is to listen to what our lives are telling us about ourselves, to hear the voice of the Holy Spirit leading us into the truth of our condition. The end of silence is to rest in God, in whom alone is one's sustenance and life. This silence is the precursor of prayer, the dialogue between the human soul and God. *Martin Israel* [4]

5 Becoming still and attentive

Experience has taught that the best way into the practice of contemplation is by way of a 'retreat'. There are many styles of retreat, some of which are quite noisy and full of activity. What we are talking about here, however, is a time spent away from the home and work environment in order to find an opportunity to be silent with God, to listen to what he has to say to us and to our world, to see something of that essential vision of God and what it means to be people of God, Godlike human beings – our true selves.

By the word 'retreat' is also meant the opportunity to *do* the work of contemplative prayer and living, not merely to listen to someone talking about it. In other words, we want to consider the kind of retreat in which we are encouraged to experience for ourselves deep and silent attention to God and to his Word, and to let his Word bear fruit in us.

Retreats arranged by the Fellowship of Contemplative Prayer put the emphasis upon the experiential and creative use of silence. There is an unwavering devotion to the biblical words of God, and the exercises are structured in such a way that the Lord's words are enabled to speak to every aspect of our human nature: to our thoughts, feelings and actions, to all that we are and all that we do. Such a retreat may be for a weekend, or last up to four days. Generally speaking we would say the longer the better; but for many people who for some very good reason just cannot get away for that length of time, to attend a quiet day which is run on the same lines can be of enormous benefit, usually leaving you longing for more.

Imagine that you are attending a Fellowship quiet day or retreat. Our purpose in this chapter is to provide some clue about what the contemplative prayer exercises will normally entail. For practical purposes, you are being addressed in a kind of double fashion – as a learner and also as a potential leader or teacher. Those of us who take the contemplative way seriously always consider ourselves as learners. But it is possible that you might at some stage be invited or required to lead a contemplative group meeting, quiet day, or even a retreat. Although we are thinking mainly about being part of a group, you, whether as learner or leader, should gain some clues about doing contemplation on your own. We have already noted that the group experience is a vital support and encouragement for what we try to do on our own day by day.

The setting

The first thing is the setting, that is, finding a setting that will enable us, as far as possible, to be still, quiet, relaxed and attentive to the Word. This is so easy to write in a book, but will prove to be for many people perhaps the most difficult part of the whole enterprise. If you are a young mother, a busy executive, or a stressed commuter with a long working day, you will immediately protest, 'Where am I going to find a still and quiet setting for contemplation?' No one can answer that question for you. For those who are determined enough to make a start, opportunities often present themselves. We shall return later to the problems of trying to lead the contemplative life in the context of home and work where ideal settings are hard to come by. For the time being, let us assume that you are lucky enough to get away from pressures of home and work to a place of quiet retreat. So we now need to know how to make the best of an ideal situation.

The best setting is a quiet room or chapel, warm and draught-free without being stuffy, and large enough for each person to have ample space. Chairs should be armless, padded or with seat cushions so that people can sit upright with feet placed flat on the floor. It is usually helpful to have a visual focus. In a chapel, there is likely to be an altar and some Christian symbol. In an ordinary meeting room, a cross or some flowers may be placed on a table. Sometimes, if the windows are low enough, a sufficient visual focus may be found outside in the garden or countryside.

People will be facing more or less in the same direction, but this is more by custom than by necessity. If the space is sufficient, people should be free to place their chairs however they please. You might want to consider sitting in a circle, or the Leader may suggest this, and have a suitable artefact placed centrally as a visual focus selected for the exercise. There can, however, sometimes be a problem with this arrangement, because eye contact with people sitting opposite can become a distraction when praying contemplatively. When speaking, the Leader [1] may want to stand to one side or behind the group, rather than face on, knowing that he or she is there to be heard rather than seen. Care will need to be exercised to ensure that those who are hard of hearing are in a position to hear. The use of modern loop systems and microphones can be of great benefit.

The posture

Although sitting upright is a customary posture to adopt for contemplation, it is by no means the only one. Once again having regard to the limitations of space, people should be free to adopt any posture that enables them to be relaxed and, at the same time, fully attentive to the Word of God. We are of course talking about the group situation here, but most of what is being said applies equally to you if you are on your own at home or in some other quiet spot of your choosing.

So let us continue talking about the discipline of bodily posture. You might like to try it out as we proceed. We need to sit in such a way that we are not unnecessarily distracted by our bodies. Our clothing and footwear should be loose and comfortable. Some people prefer not to wear shoes at all.

Whether we decide to use a chair, meditation stool, kneeler or the carpeted floor itself, it is best to sit straight but never stiffly or rigidly. The spine is not like a ramrod: it has a gentle curve. Be aware of that curve, and sit comfortably and relaxed. The head should rest centrally on the spinal column and not be allowed to settle into the shoulders. The feet and knees should be about shoulder-width apart. This is one reason why women usually prefer to wear trousers or long skirts.

It is best to place the hands lightly and loosely on the thighs, and allow the whole body to take on an attitude of openness. It is rather like a flower opening itself to the sun. It is as if we were saying to God: 'Here I am, open and ready to receive whatever you have to say or give to me in the silence.' We may also liken our bodily attitude to the young Samuel, who said to his Lord: 'Speak, Lord, for your servant is listening' (1 Samuel 3:9).

One of the most useful aids both to relaxation and to the kind of concentration needed for the prayer of stillness and silence is controlled breathing. Having relaxed the muscular frame of the body as far as you are able, take two or three really deep breaths, in, and out. After that, just be aware of your breathing for a few moments as you breathe a little more deeply and a little more slowly than usual. The word 'inspiration' means 'in-breathing' or being breathed into. Breath is itself a powerful biblical image signifying the Spirit of God which is at work in creation, and also in the re-creation inaugurated by Jesus who breathed on his disciples after the Resurrection (John 20:22). So as we breathe slowly and deeply (but without strain) we may momentarily think of ourselves as being 'breathed into' by the Holy Spirit as a preparation for receiving the Spirit and Life of the Word.

The struggle

So far in this chapter we have dealt with the setting for contemplation, the importance of a disciplined bodily posture, and the value of controlled breathing. This physical aspect of the discipline will not necessarily be achieved easily. Like everything else to do with contemplation, we may experience a terrible struggle in our desire to *be* still, to *be* relaxed, to *be* open, to *be* attentive. There may even be some significant physical reasons for this struggle, for example, if you happen to be physically disabled in some way, or have real difficulty in breathing. It may thus be impossible to sit in the way described. All we can say is that, unless you are actually experiencing severe pain, be encouraged to work within your personal limitations, knowing that others are alongside you in the struggle.

But the fruit of bodily discipline – of a still, relaxed, open and attentive posture – makes every bit of the struggle worthwhile. It will also inevitably have a beneficial effect upon our mental and emotional condition. We tend to find that the still, relaxed posture gradually enables us to cope with the stress and tension in our lives and not to be destroyed by them. Not that the authentic Christian way of life is about getting rid of all stress and tension.[2] A prime symbol for the Christian contemplative is not a calm pond with a floating lily, but a cross: a cross which represents enormous but totally creative stress and tension. The contemplative tends gradually to develop an inner strength which enables him to live with the stress and tension calmly and use it creatively. This includes whatever personal mess and muddle we may be in – whatever sins may be plaguing us. The contemplative way is simply to keep whatever strain or pressure we may be under, whatever worries or disappointments we may have, wide open before God in a deliberate attitude of quiet, relaxed attention. By resting in God we tend to cope with the stress and strain better than most, and to break down less easily.

What if we have subjected ourselves to an intolerable degree of stress and tension because up to now we have not begun to find our rest in God? What if the strain has broken us? What if we have suffered, say, a nervous breakdown or heart attack, perhaps because of work overload (or lack of work), unrealistic goals, living too much by the clock, personality clashes, marital problems, rootlessness?

That brokenness can be used creatively. The Cross or the eucharistic bread reveal Jesus as a broken person. In fact, properly understood, the contemplative way is about being broken in order to be remade. 'Are not MY words,' asks God, 'like a hammer that shatters rock?' (Jeremiah 23:29, REB). That is a sign of hope for us all and for the world. Contemplation allows the hammer of God's love gently to chip away, to break us down, and to do it creatively, not destructively. It is a joy to see people who have been leading a self-destructive existence at last finding their rest in God.[3] It is not just playing with words to say that a breakdown can be a time of exciting break-*through*.

Some teachers of meditation talk as though *all* stress and tension were bad for us. Such teaching is dangerous nonsense. It produces flabby people who are disengaged from the tough reality of living. What is needed is a disciplined life which includes obedience to God's command to come to him (which can then be understood as his welcoming invitation rather than peremptory order), to be still and to rest in him, to let him take the burden which is us and ours, and to enable him to empower us for that stretching and breaking which is an inevitable part of real living.

The invitation

In a retreat, the setting, postures and breathing disciplines help us to begin to be quiet and relaxed. But the Lord's own words can lead us towards a deeper, inner sense of stillness and rest:

'Come to ME, all whose work is hard, whose load is heavy; and I will give you rest' (Matthew 11:28, NEB).

'Come with ME . . . to some lonely place where you can rest quietly' (Mark 6:31, NEB).

'Be still, and know that I AM God' (Psalm 46:10, AV).

'Keep silence before ME' (Isaiah 41:1, NEB).

'In stillness and in staying quiet, there lies your strength'

(Isaiah 30:15, NEB).

These are just a handful of many similar biblical phrases. Every single word is spoken out of loving desire for our well-being. They sound like a gentle invitation. But, like much of the Word, they bear the force of a command – a command to be obeyed, for our own good and for the glory of God: *'Come . . . Be* still . . . *Keep* silent . . . *Get* some rest.'

As each retreatant sits silently with a disciplined posture, he or she is encouraged to feed upon or drink in such words. The leader will begin by repeating the full text, for example, 'Come to me, all whose work is hard, whose load is heavy, and I will give you rest' (perhaps using an older version, *Come unto me all you who labour and are heavy laden and I will give you rest*). The leader then gradually reduces this saying of Jesus to its bare and basic essentials, for instance, 'Come to me and I will give you rest . . . Come . . . and rest'.

Retreatants will be invited mentally to repeat these words in the silence, paying loving attention to them, focusing on them, allowing them to become the centre of the stillness. When this happens, you begin to realise that it is not you who speak the words; it is the Lord himself speaking them to you. This will become the preface to a whole new experience of listening at depth to the Word of God being spoken to us and within us. The retreat is the ideal setting, but as we have already seen, you can in theory listen to the Word at any time and in any place. In practice, of course, it may not be so easy.

One final piece of advice before we move on. It is not a good idea to try to contemplate immediately after a meal, particularly if you have eaten heartily. The processes of digestion will necessarily diminish the ability required in contemplative praying to concentrate and focus mentally and spiritually. In retreats, afternoons are usually reserved as free time for this reason, for it can be harmful to the digestion, just as if you engage in swimming or other strenuous activity too soon after eating. In other contexts, whether at prayer group meetings, quiet days, or engaging in solo contemplation at home or elsewhere, this injunction will need to be modified according to circumstances. No harm will come if you contemplate after a light snack, but it is always sensible to leave as much time as possible between the end of a meal and the start of contemplative 'work'.

6 Distractions, positive and negative

In this chapter, we are still thinking in terms of a group of people who have come together to explore contemplation – to share the experience of contemplative prayer and life, whether in the context of someone's home, a monthly meeting, a quiet day or a silent retreat. Again, it will be relevant to what you may try to do on your own.

Let us assume that the group and its individual members have become still, quiet, relaxed, attentive. Each one has adopted a disciplined, yet relaxed posture, whether seated or otherwise – open to God, as flowers are open towards the light and warmth of the sun.

The room or chapel is unlikely to be altogether silent. External noise will almost certainly intrude: the noise of traffic, road works, children at play, animals, birds. Internal noise may also invade the silence: the heating system, a ticking clock, a creaking chair, a sneeze or cough, a rumbling stomach – even perhaps a snore! Most of these things are only momentary and minor distractions. If someone should fall soundly asleep and snore audibly, let them! That person falls to sleep because he or she *needs* to. Let them sleep off their tiredness and *then* they will be able to give themselves to the demanding work of contemplative prayer.

Distractions will always plague our attempts to pay attention to God and his Word. Some of those distractions are, we might say, the very devil. To use traditional language, the more we try to pay loving attention to God, the more the devil dislikes it and tries to distract us from God. It has often been found at a contemplative retreat that what appears to be an ideal setting in quiet rural surroundings suddenly and unaccountably becomes a focus for distracting noise: a lawnmower starts up; a tractor decides to cultivate the adjacent field; the builders they have been expecting for weeks suddenly turn up to do repairs just as you start a contemplative exercise.

Possibly the most difficult of devilish distractions are those described by Robert Llewllyn as 'voluntary' (see his pamphlet, *The Positive Role of Distraction in Prayer*, published by SLG Press, 1977). These are the ones which we deliberately allow to distract us, the sort we are inclined to wallow in. They may take the form of mild daydreaming, sometimes sensual or sexual fantasy. In fact, a whole range of defiling, destructive, devilish thoughts and feelings can invade our times of silent attention to God.[1]

Another insidious kind of distraction from contemplation is sheer frustration and boredom: a sense that the exercise is getting nowhere and is not really worth the time and effort; a sense that it is not really doing anything for us or for anyone else, not helping us to grow spiritually; a sense that the whole thing is one big con-trick and utterly boring.

Equally insidious are distractions at the other end of the spectrum: a sense that everything in the garden is lovely; that everything is warm and cosy; that there is the scent of real progress and success; that our minds and hearts are expanding in all directions; that the whole enterprise is one big turn-on. What a temptation this can be: to wallow in the warm, sweet-scented garden, enjoying the various sensations instead of giving undivided attention to the Word!

Such distractions may be occasional or they may be chronic, even pathological. You may need to share such problems with your 'wider fellowship' and certainly with your spiritual director or guide. In one way or another, distractions need to be put in their proper place.

A story from personal experience may be helpful at this point. I used to be a professional French horn player, accustomed to the concert platform. One evening, the brass, woodwind and percussion were totally silent. The strings of the orchestra were playing Elgar's beautiful *Sospiri*. The standard of performance was exceptionally high. Apart from the sound of the strings, every single person was still, silent, enraptured.

Without warning, from somewhere up in a balcony there came an almighty 'Bang!' Someone had slammed a door. Everyone, players and audience alike, was totally distracted. The string music fell to pieces and petered out. The conductor was visibly shaken. Every face in the hall turned towards the direction from which the noise had come. In a few seconds, the place was buzzing with angry or amused chatter. The horn section succumbed to helpless laughter.

What a mess! But we had a job of work to do: a piece of music to perform. The only thing was for everyone present to get back deliberately to the work of paying attention, to focus attention on conductor or orchestra, to reject the intrusion and listen to Elgar's music.

In contemplation it is our intention to be giving our total, rapt attention to the Word. Distraction *will* invade our silent attention. There will be times even of chaos. The action to take is not to prolong distractions but to get back to the job in hand – deliberately to re-focus attention on the Word. As Brother Roger of Taizé said, it is all part of the 'struggle to become still enough to reflect the face of God'.

It surprises some people to discover that distractions are not necessarily destructive. They can be used positively and creatively, to help us to be more disciplined in the quality of our attention to God. In fact, without distractions, the word 'attention' would be meaningless.

There is another class of distraction. These are the sort we cannot possibly help: the sort that may need even urgent action before we can give undivided attention to the Word. A lady jumped up in the middle of a contemplative group meeting in great alarm. She was most apologetic, but she would just have to leave: she had put a chicken in the oven, was sure she had left the oven on high, and there was no one in the house!

Something that we have forgotten to do, especially if it is important, can be very distracting indeed. It may not be as urgent as the chicken episode, but it may need noting down in writing so that it doesn't get forgotten again. When you are trying to contemplate on your own, it is not a bad idea to have a pencil and some paper near by, not for noting down thoughts and ideas, but simply to use if you are suddenly distracted by something important that you must not forget when the silent time is over.

There is another subtle kind of distraction which may be considered rather as an interruption. Imagine for a moment that you are having a serious conversation with someone. At this or that point, you are meant to be doing the listening, paying proper attention to what the other person is saying. But there is something in your nature which will not let you simply listen in silence. You keep interrupting. It may only be the odd word or two: 'Yes', 'No', 'I understand', 'I have every sympathy with that', 'I think that's brilliant', 'You're right', and so on.

A good counsellor knows that such interruptions are both impolite and unhelpful. They are impolite because, whatever we may fondly imagine about ourselves, we are not giving the other person the total attention he or she deserves.

Contemplation is made of the same stuff. We are not giving undivided attention to God's Word if we are interjecting our own bits of chatter. We may be wanting to say things that ultimately must be said – but not now. We may want to utter the language of adoration, praise, thanksgiving – but not now. Contemplation is just being naked before God, totally exposed to him and to his penetrating Word. It is being silent and letting him do the talking he wants to do.

The great strength of the method advocated and practised by the Fellowship of Contemplative Prayer is that the

Fellowship uses as food for the silence only what are technically called the 'dominical words' or Sayings of scripture: only the words or Sayings which are represented as coming from the Lord's own mouth, the Word or words spoken by the Lord, in the first person. As the rest of the chapter will show, they are just right for dealing with distractions.

Some of the Sayings have already been referred to – some of the words by which the Lord calls us to rest in him. But in fact the Bible is endlessly rich in the language of God spoken directly and clearly to his people – inexhaustibly rich in words and phrases that come from the mouth of God and which are food for contemplative prayer.

Here are just a few examples to be going on with. Later, we will explore the use of similar phrases, in the context of a full contemplative prayer exercise. As you look at these examples, take a little while to ponder over them and try straight away to capture something of their potential, something of their spirit and life, something of that essential nature of God and of human nature at its best. As we have seen, every Word of God is a Word to live by; every Word a seed for sowing in the human mind and heart and will; every Word an expression of the Lord's loving desire that we should know him and co-operate with him; every Word, according to the time and occasion when it is heard at depth, providing a spiritual diet of milk and honey, or having the power to scorch and burn, or to give a fine cutting edge.

These 'I AM' phrases, or Sayings, speak of the nature of God: 'I AM holy . . .' (Leviticus 20:7, NEB), 'I AM full of compassion . . .' (Exodus 22:27, NEB), 'I AM filled with tenderness . . .' (Jeremiah 31:20, NEB), 'I AM full of strength and power . . .' (Micah 3:8, NEB), 'I AM the Good Shepherd . . .' (John 10:11, AV), 'I AM the light of the world' (John 9:5, AV).

Some of these are from the Old Testament and some from the New. By feeding silently upon such phrases, by letting them live and grow in the mind and heart, by letting them motivate the will, we suddenly or slowly make a far-reaching discovery. Not only do we begin to catch a glimpse of who God is, we also begin to see something of who *we* truly are – something of our *own* essential Godlike nature. In God, we begin to find our true self and our true goal. For example, if I am true to God and true to myself – if I am truly human – then I must own and live by the spirit of the 'I AM' Sayings. I must be holy, full of compassion and tenderness, strength and power. I must be a good shepherd and light for the world.

Note carefully that the 'I AM' Sayings give us only a *glimpse* of God's nature and of our own nature. If we could liken God to a glorious jewel which has endless facets, each of the many 'I AM' Sayings represents only one of those facets of God's nature. Even then, we can catch only a tiny glimpse which in itself can become brighter than the brightest sun, so that we realise we cannot see God at all. Even if we were to spend a lifetime and more than a lifetime contemplating just one of the 'I AM' Sayings, we would never exhaust its significance for our understanding of God and of ourselves. It would simply lead us inevitably to the conclusion that whatever words we may be receiving, they are nothing more than fumbling attempts to express the inexpressible – to utter the unutterable. In the end, God says, 'I AM WHO I AM' (Exodus 3:14, RSV), beyond all description. Again, what is true of God is also true of every human being: I am who I am, defying all attempts to wrap me up, label me, and stick me in some pigeon-hole. I am, like God, beyond all description. I am who I am; part of the divine mystery of being.

It should be said at this stage that not every single first person utterance represented as proceeding from the mouth of God is necessarily suitable for contemplative purposes. The selecting of suitable dominical Sayings is something of a skill or an art, and comes more easily as you gain experience in the way of contemplation. Generally speaking, Sayings that are best suited for contemplative prayer are those which relate to the great themes of the Bible such as the self-revelation of God and his purposes, creation, election, salvation, sin and forgiveness, the meaning of suffering, death and resurrection, the end of time. Such Sayings will usually have a host of cross-references, for these great themes run like golden threads through the whole Bible from Genesis to Revelation. In addition, many (perhaps most) of the Old Testament dominical Sayings that are suitable for contemplation, will sound as if they could have been spoken by Jesus himself in the course of his teaching and preaching ministry. The 'good news' of the New Testament is witnessed to in ample terms in the Old. 'I AM holy . . . full of compassion and tenderness . . . full of strength and power'. Sayings such as these speak with incisive clarity from the heart of the Cross, as if from the lips of Jesus.

In addition to the 'I AM' Sayings, there are hosts of others cast in the first person. For example, there are the 'I will' Sayings: 'I will come to you', 'I will be with you', 'I will strengthen you'; there are the 'I have' Sayings: 'I have chosen you', 'I, the Lord, have spoken and I will act', 'I have loved you with an everlasting love'; the 'MY' Sayings: 'MY love will never be withdrawn', 'MY eyes stream with tears', 'MY servant, in whom I delight'; the 'ME' Sayings: 'Come to ME', 'Come back to ME, for I AM patient with you', 'Trust in ME'; there are other very direct words of command from the Lord: 'Choose life', 'Be perfect', 'Do not be afraid'; and there are the searching questions of God: 'Where are you?', 'What are you doing here?', 'Do you believe that I can heal you?'.[2]

In writing this chapter, I am aware of being one among many, both in and beyond the Fellowship of Contemplative Prayer, who have been using these Sayings and others like them in silent contemplation for years. They penetrate the centre of one's being and become a sort of reservoir – a resource for Christian living. They are the Word which becomes flesh, embodied, as it were, in humanity. However stubborn and rebellious we are – whatever kind of resistance we put up – if we place ourselves in the Lord's presence and listen to him, his words do sink in and bear fruit. The Word becomes, even imperceptibly, part of our own mental and emotional equipment. This miraculous process shows the truth of the Word spoken through Isaiah the prophet:

> 'MY Word,' says God, 'is like the snow and the rain that come down from the sky to water the earth. They make the crops grow and provide seed for sowing and food to eat. So also will be the Word that I speak – it will not fail to do what I plan for it; it will do everything I send it to do.' *(Isaiah 55:10–11, TEV)*

This process of embodying the Word also indicates the truth of Jesus' saying: 'The water I give . . . will become . . . a spring of water welling up to eternal life' (John 4:14, NIV). So the Lord is saying, in and through the contemplative, 'I AM', 'I will', 'I have', 'MY', 'ME'; he it is who speaks the word of command to 'Choose' and 'Be' and 'Do'; he it is who probes with searching questions about where I am, what I am doing here, and whether I have confidence in his power to heal.

The founder of the Fellowship of Contemplative Prayer often ended his personal letters: 'With as much love as I have so far received'. He would have said that he had hardly scratched the surface – hardly begun to be filled with all the fullness of God's love. That will only happen when we have become totally saturated with the Word; when we have reached the full stature of Christ; when we finally reflect the splendid, glorious, majestic, radiant face of God. Until then, we plod on with the patient work of contemplation, dealing with the inevitable and endless distractions, exposing ourselves more and more to the penetrating words of God, allowing them to work in us and ultimately through us, enabling us to be truly human.

7   Get stuck in!

This rather brutal title is intended to jolt you out of the temptation to read about prayer rather than to do it. It may be helpful to read a book about swimming or driving a car, but the only real way to learn is to get into the water, or behind the steering wheel and get stuck in. The same is true of prayer; and once you get going and are determined to stick at it, you will find that God's Holy Spirit is becoming your teacher. You will learn as much, if not more, by apparent failure as by apparent success. I use the word 'apparent' advisedly, for ultimately there can be no failure for those who are seeking to build their relationship with God. He will see to that. From your perspective, things will go well or badly in your praying as they do in day-to-day life. There will be blessings and rewards; there will also be trials and agonies to endure.

When things go well, and God seems close, and you feel good, then simply be thankful. When prayer becomes fraught with difficulty and God seems far off or even non-existent and you are tempted to give up, still be thankful. For you are probably learning more from the bad times than from the good. Every child learns to walk by stumbling. The founder of the Fellowship of Contemplative Prayer, Robert Coulson, was fond of repeating, 'There is only one failure in prayer, and that is to stop trying.' This is why he wisely worded the Rule for Members 'I undertake . . . to commit myself *as far as I am able* . . .' Another spiritual writer, David Torkington, has this to say about trying in prayer:

I have been stressing the word 'trying', but in Christian spirituality the way in which a person tries is more important still. If trying is the heart of prayer, then gentleness is the soul of prayer. The gentle way in which you start again, no matter how many times you fail in prayer, breathes the breath of humility into the very way in which you try. It is the humility of one who knows their weakness, knows that they will fail time and time again, but is never deterred from starting anew no matter how many times they may fall.

It is the arrogant person who is angered by failure, who knits their brow, grits their teeth and clenches their fists in an endeavour to batter down the gates of heaven. They are angry, not because they have failed God, but because they have failed themselves, and the great ideas that they have set up for themselves. Whenever you find yourself getting angry with your failure in prayer, be sure that it is your own pride that has been injured. The humble person is never surprised by failure, nor do they delay in beginning again to turn back to the only One who can bring strength out of weakness.

What is true of prayer is true of the whole of the spiritual journey. We are all sinners, and we will fall until the day we die. Success does not consist in not falling, so much as in continually getting up. It's all in the getting up, or more precisely in the gentle way in which we get off the ground to start again, sorry for having fallen but never surprised.[1]

We have seen that the essence of contemplative prayer is to allow the Word of God to 'dwell in you richly' (Colossians 3:16, AV). This chapter will tell you how to set about this in the simplest possible way, both by yourself and with other people. For all that it is simple, the method is profound theologically, philosophically and psychologically – *theologically*, because it is based on the dynamic relationship between God and humankind; *philosophically*, because it engages the mind and is linked with the traditional search for wisdom (*Sophia*) and the meaning of life; *psychologically*, because it directs our will and influences our attitudes and our behaviour. Some of what follows has already been touched on, but I make no apology for the repetition because our subject is of such significance and importance that we often need to go over the same ground and approach it from a slightly different direction.

On your own

I will assume at the moment that you are a complete novice. If you are not, please don't skip the rest of this chapter. Time and again, those of us who have been practising this way in prayer for years find that we have a need to go right back to the beginning and start again. During our spiritual pilgrimage, our journey into God, I doubt if many, if any, of us should remove our 'L' plates in this life.

Whether you belong to a prayer group or not, or even a religious community, much of your contemplative praying will have to be solo. In order to receive the words of God as fully as possible, it is important to be able to relax physically and mentally and thus to reduce tension. Just as the sky cannot be reflected in troubled waters, so the presence of God cannot be felt by a restless soul. Relaxing in the proper way does not mean simply taking one's ease. Archbishop Anthony Bloom, who was one of the twentieth century's greatest authorities on prayer, has a helpful military analogy as he writes about silent prayer:

> The real silence we must aim at as a starting point is a complete repose of mind, heart and will, the complete silence of all that is in us including our body . . . so we may be completely aware of the Word we are receiving, completely alert yet in complete repose. The Silence I am speaking of is the silence of the sentry on duty, at a critical moment, alert, immobile, poised yet alive to every movement, every sound.

We have already outlined the way to become still and attentive in body and mind in chapter 5, but here is a brief résumé. Find a moment when you have at least ten clear minutes undisturbed. Choose a chair which is comfortable but upright (best without arms and not too 'saggy'). Sit comfortably but with the head and spine in as straight a line as possible. Slow down the rate of breathing and breathe a little more deeply than usual. Sit relaxed but alert; close the eyes or fix them on a point in the middle distance.

Having become outwardly and inwardly still and receptive, allow yourself two minutes in which to respond to the Lord's invitation to come to him. Hear these words being spoken by him to you: 'Come unto ME all you who labour and are heavy laden, and I will give you rest' (Matthew 11:28). Reach inwards, taking to our Lord any pains, fears, suffering, sins or troubles of the day.

After this short period of self-examination we are ready to receive the chosen Word. Select a short I AM Saying from the last chapter (or one from the list at the end of this chapter). Having learnt it by heart, repeat it slowly over and over again in your mind, and without trying to think about the words; just let the words sink in.

It is important not to overdo it at first. This form of prayer is not a striving and an effort, but just being there, quietly attentive. When you are more used to it, the silence can be lengthened, or another short period of the day may be devoted to it. If possible, recall the sentence momentarily at other times during the day, especially last thing at night before going to sleep, and first thing on waking.

Repeat this exercise daily for a period of time, a week, a fortnight, perhaps even for a month; then take another Saying and begin again. As you become more accustomed to this way in prayer, and if you are able to devote more time to it, you may want to structure your time along the lines outlined in the next section about praying with other people. You may also find that you are able to hold several Sayings in your memory and switch from one to another. It is not a good idea to do this during the course of a single contemplative exercise, but over a period of time, say, a month, you might have used half a dozen different Sayings. Sometimes the use of a particular Saying is dictated by personal circumstances, or because you feel guided to intercede for particular people or concerns.

It is always a good idea to keep a notebook and write down a list of Sayings. I remember from schooldays, we were taught to have a vocabulary notebook in which we wrote down new words and their meanings. When you write down Dominical or I AM Sayings as you use them, or come across them in your Bible reading, you are building up your Divine Vocabulary which will become a ready source of Words from the Lord which you can call on both for your contemplative prayer-time and at other times.

Praying with other people

Praying on your own is an essential part of anyone's spiritual pilgrimage, but very few of us are called to solitary prayer on a permanent basis. We are created for fellowship and relationship one with another: as an African proverb puts it very succinctly, 'A man is a man by reason of other men'. In traditional Christian terms, belonging to a church ensures the connectedness which is needed for spiritual health. The Church is the context in which we experience the fellowship of the Holy Spirit. Within that context, many people find additional strength and encouragement in the smaller groups which form for study and prayer of various kinds as a kind of supplement to the main spiritual diet, rather as an aperitif or after-dinner coffee supplements a main meal.

In following the way of the prayer of stillness, I can hardly recommend strongly enough the desirability of being part of a contemplative prayer group. Such a group is always more than the mere sum of its members. The Saying of Jesus immediately springs to mind: 'Where two or three are gathered together in my name, there I AM in the midst' (Matthew 18:20). The term *group* is perhaps a misnomer, because the Lord's words need to be taken quite literally: *two or three*. In contemplative prayer, the success of a group is never measured by the numbers who attend. If you can find even one friend or partner with whom to share an hour of contemplative silence on a regular basis, then the spiritual value of the exercise will be significantly enhanced. And it probably won't be long before you find some others wanting to join in. So whenever the word *group* is used in this chapter, please take it to mean any number from two upwards.

Prayer group meeting

I now want to show you how a typical meeting of a prayer group of the Fellowship of Contemplative Prayer is organised, whose focus is on the prayer of silence, listening contemplatively to the Word of God in the way described in this book. Clearly this is just one of a number of ways that people can pray in groups; but it is a way that has proved itself to be of great value since it was introduced by the founder of the Fellowship, Robert Coulson, in the middle of the last century.

The group meets regularly, weekly, fortnightly or monthly in a convenient location. It may be a church or chapel or meeting room; often it is in someone's home. It may be in the morning, or afternoon, or evening, and it tends to be in the same place each time. This is because you can settle down to a pattern of prayer much more readily in surroundings that are familiar; to chop and change the venue can be an unnecessary distraction. The running or ordering of a prayer group will vary according to the numbers who normally come. For our purposes, I am going to assume an average attendance of about ten. You can easily adapt the system if there are more or fewer than that.

There will normally be one person who is responsible for convening the group: a prayer group secretary. The secretary will keep details of all the members, names, addresses and phone numbers, and perhaps e-mail addresses too. They will ensure that the venue (it may be their own or another member's home, if not the church or some other meeting place) is adequately prepared with sufficient chairs. They may also see to it that there is some refreshment on hand after the meeting for those who want to stay behind for a chat.

At the start of the meeting, the secretary will give a brief welcome, especially to any newcomers. With an attendance of ten, there will probably be another four or five people who for various reasons will have had to give apologies, and the secretary will say who they are. They will also report on anyone who is in need of special prayer, or any other concern for the group's intercessions; and they will invite other members to do the same. They will then probably introduce the person (or people; it might be two) who has been chosen to lead the session.

Witnessing the Word of God

Here I just need to digress a little to explain the function of the leader of a Fellowship contemplative prayer group. We avoid the words *leader* or *conductor* and instead use the term *Witness of the Word of God*, or just *Witness* for short. For that is precisely what the person is who is called to lead others in this kind of praying; a witness of God's Word. Such a person will be well versed in the Scriptures and prepared to open out, or unpack, the particular Saying that has been selected for the meeting. Theirs is a very particular task; briefly, to enable themselves and the other members of the group to be able to listen more effectively and attentively to the Word which is spoken from the Divine Source.

It is not easy to say in so many words exactly how the Witness is to fulfil his or her task, for it is a skill that comes with practice. It is easier to say what the rôle of Witness is *not*. Although the Saying needs to be illumined by placing it in its biblical context and exploring relevant cross-references, the Witness is not called on to give a Bible study. Nor is Witnessing the Word an opportunity for preaching (clergy and lay preachers please note!). Witnessing must by definition be *theo-logical*, for it is dealing with the word (*logos*) of God (*theos*); but this is not the time for deep theological thinking or exposition. Nor need the Witness demonstrate their breadth of knowledge about the mystical tradition or the great spiritual giants of the past. Of course, occasional reference to such authorities may be helpful, but the touch must be light and the language straightforward.

In brief, a Witness in our terms is a person who, in contemplation, has personally already been moved, grasped, and challenged in their mind, heart and will by the Word of God, in particular by the Saying chosen for the meeting, and is ready to share some of the insights they have gained from their own experience.

So let us now return to the meeting. With the preliminaries over, the Witness will introduce the first silence with the Saying from Matthew: 'Come unto me all you who labour and are heavy laden, and I will give you rest' (Matthew 11:28, AV).[2] This gives us an opportunity, during a two-minute period of silence, to off-load any burdens of care or anxiety we may be carrying. The Witness will then give a brief outline of the meaning and significance of the chosen Saying to prepare our minds to receive the Word with a little more understanding. This will only be for a few minutes, and then there will be silence for up to ten minutes during which we will seek to receive the Saying into our minds, by slow and careful silent mental repetition.

The Witness breaks gently into the silence by repeating the Saying aloud, and spends a few minutes exploring something of the *feeling* side of the Saying, becoming more anecdotal and less theological in what he or she says about it. It is worth repeating here a favourite word of Robert Coulson's. He taught that the Witness should consider their own words as mere 'patter', like the words of a conjuror which are inconsequential compared with the actual trick. For what is important in any group contemplative exercise is not the words of the Witness, but the *Word of God spoken in the silence.* For that reason, incidentally, Coulson was not very happy about people taking notes while he himself was Witnessing the Word.

So this second few minutes of 'patter' is to prepare us to receive the Saying more deeply into our hearts during the next ten minutes or so of silence. As our mind has been informed by the Word during the previous silence, so now our heart, the more deeply *inward* part of our nature, is impregnated by God's Word which is spirit and life. As we once again mentally repeat the Saying, we become more aware of that Saying being spoken to us, or within us, by the Lord himself. This is a precious time, and many people have spoken about the profound feeling of being indwelt by the Spirit through the Word during this second period of group silence. At this deeper level of contemplative prayer, we are indeed gaining *heart-knowledge* of the Lord who calls himself I AM.

We may not, however, rest there. To have the mind and the heart filled by the Word, but not to have the *will* also engaged is to leave our prayer in an unstable condition, rather like a person trying to sit on a two-legged stool. So our Witness will once again intrude on the silence, and then gently lead us in the third part of our contemplative exercise, which is the receiving of the Word into our will, and the use of the Saying as a watchword and in intercession. As we experience how the Word of God interacts with our own being, so we believe that we may share this rich blessing with others, by speaking the Word to them *in the Name of God I AM*.

During the time that remains for our exercise, we have a twin focus of attention. We remain mindful of the Saying, and at the same time we bring into the silence those people and concerns for whom we need to pray. We know that God is speaking his life-giving Word not just to ourselves but to everyone, indeed to the whole creation which depends on the Word for its very being and well-being. In intercession, it is as if we are being used gently to remind others of this truth by speaking the Word to them, or hearing it on their behalf. This part of the exercise, though difficult to describe, is greatly meaningful for those who engage in it. Space will not allow a fuller explanation, but if you want to know more, then you may make enquiries to the Fellowship (details are in the Appendix).

Our contemplative exercise will have lasted just one hour, and in conclusion, the Witness will say a prayer to thank God for the bountiful riches of the Spirit which he pours out as light pours from the sun, and to rededicate ourselves in his service.[3] At this point, some people may like to leave the meeting quietly, or may have to go about other duties. Often, people stay for some refreshment and conversation before going. In any case, all who take part in a contemplative prayer group have a keen sense that they have truly been engaged in the Lord's work. They have opened themselves to the spirit and life of God's Word, having been in direct communication with the Divine Source of that Word; and they have a real sense of being used as channels or reflectors of the Word, in some indefinable way being able to convey its light and life-giving power to places and people where it is most needed.

Who can witness the Word of God?

If I were to answer that question by saying 'Anyone can' I should not be far from the truth. Most contemplative prayer groups such as the one I have just been writing about work on a sort of do-it-yourself basis. Members take it in turns; sometimes they may work in pairs. If I were to Witness the Word at the next meeting, I should want to select the Saying about a month beforehand, so that I could use it in my own contemplative prayer times.

Let's suppose I was choosing the words of Jesus, 'I am the Resurrection and the Life' from John 11:25. First of all, I would probably find some thoughts about this coming into my mind as a result of my own contemplation of the Saying, and I would jot these down. I would also read the whole of John, Chapter 11 in order to set the Saying in its context. As I use a cross-reference Bible, I would look up some of the cross-references. My Bible reading would give me some more ideas to note down. I might also look at a Bible commentary on John's Gospel. If I was still short of ideas, I might ask the minister in my own church for any thoughts he or she may have about the Saying. This work should provide me with enough material to prepare my own commentary to last about five to seven minutes, i.e. sufficient to introduce the first silence for the contemplative exercise.

As we saw, the commentary introducing the second period of silence needs to be more personal and anecdotal, for it addresses our feelings rather than our intellect. I would want to make some notes about the positive and joyful aspect of a truly Christian attitude to dying and death. I would remember that this Saying prefaces every Christian funeral service. I would share any memory of the joy of the Easter faith, and my personal feelings about the assurances of the gospel regarding eternal life.

It stands to reason that some people will find that they have a greater facility than others for Witnessing the Word of God in this way. The Fellowship of Contemplative Prayer has some very experienced Witnesses among its members and can provide training for people who want to learn, or to learn more about it and you are welcome to ask for information from the sources listed (see the Appendix).

Adapting the method

There is no doubt that the hour-long contemplative exercise divided into the three parts that I have just outlined is the most satisfactory way of using this method. It is widely used in prayer groups, and if you were to attend a Fellowship retreat or Quiet Day, this is what you would experience. You may, however, need to adapt it to suit your own quiet times. When you are on your own, your personal 'Witnessing of the Word' is your spiritual reading and meditation. When you enter into silent prayer, it is always best to begin with two minutes of listening to the Divine Invitation, 'Come unto me . . .' etc., from Matthew 11:28. Then you can immediately focus on your chosen Saying and allow the receiving of the Word into the mind and heart to follow each other without a break.

Always move towards intercession at the end of the time you have available. The threefold structure involving the mind, the heart and the will is spiritually important, because we are told to love both God *and* our neighbour. It is also psychologically satisfactory to engage our whole thinking, feeling and acting self when we are at prayer as we do in our ordinary living. We are often moved to pray for other people or concerns as the first part of prayer, but that is far from ideal. You cannot give without having first received, any more than you can give someone a drink from an empty jug. Contemplative prayer ensures that we get the sequence in the right order, first of all receiving a measure of God's loving-kindness, and then sharing it with others. St Bernard of Clairvaux puts it very succinctly: 'If you are wise, you will consider yourself as a reservoir rather than as a canal. For a canal spreads abroad the water it receives, but a reservoir waits until it is filled before overflowing and thus communicates without loss to itself its superabundant water.' That is a very precise image of contemplative intercession.

Some suggested Bible 'words' for contemplation

'I AM with you always' (Matthew 28:20, RSV).

'MY peace I give unto you' (John 14:27, AV).

'I have loved you with an everlasting love' (Jeremiah 31:3, AV).

'These things have I spoken to you, that MY joy might remain in you, and that your joy might be full' (John 15:11, AV).

'Fear nothing, for I AM with you . . . be not afraid for I AM your God' (Isaiah 41:10, NEB).

'Be still: and know that I AM God' (Psalm 46:10, AV).

'MY words shall never pass away; they are spirit and they are life' (Mark 13:31; John 6:63, NEB).

'Abide in ME and I in you' (John 15:4, AV).

'I AM the Lord that healeth thee' (Exodus 15:26, AV).

'I have come that you might have life, and have it in all its fullness' (John 10:10, REB).

'I will go before you, and make the crooked places straight' (Isaiah 45:2, AV).

'MY grace is sufficient for you, for MY strength is made perfect in weakness' (2 Corinthians 12:9, AV).

Part
2

SIX EXERCISES

Introduction

Each of the following contemplative exercises is prepared for an hour-long session, but they can be adapted for any situation according to the various circumstances described in Chapter 7. I suggest that you are not likely to derive much, if any, benefit from silent prayer on your own unless you have at least ten uninterrupted minutes to focus on the Saying. For groups, whether meeting as a prayer group, or for a quiet day or a retreat, unless you are introducing contemplative prayer for the first time to beginners, the exercise should be timed as carefully as possible to last for just one hour. Experience has shown that an hour is a significant period of time. It seems to be more than mere chance that Jesus is recorded as having said to the disciples in Gethsemane, 'Could you not watch one hour?' (Mark 14:37, RSV).

It is usually helpful for a group to have the Saying written up in large clear letters and placed, not necessarily in the front at the dead centre, but somewhere where is it visible to all. An alternative is to have the Saying printed out. Some retreat and quiet day Witnesses of the Word will be able to provide a complete list of Sayings in advance. Another way is to have the Saying printed on small slips of paper or card, one for each person. This way they can look at them during the silences if they need a reminder, and also take them away to keep in a bag or pocket as a portable watchword for use during the week or month ahead.

8   Consider your life

Preliminary

First of all we spend two minutes silently listening to the
Divine Invitation: 'Come unto ME all you who labour and are
heavy laden, and I will give you rest' (Matthew 11:28, AV).

Consider your way of life. (Haggai 1:5, REB)

Preparing the mind

'Consider your way of life . . .' This is a prophetic Word. It
was uttered through a man named Haggai, in Jerusalem,
about 2,500 years ago. Like all authentic prophecy, it
speaks directly, clearly, incisively to you and to me: 'Consider your way of life.'

Other English versions of the Scriptures translate the
same Hebrew text in a different way: for example, 'Reflect
carefully how things have gone for you' (JB), 'Don't you see
what is happening to you?' (GNB) 'Give careful thought to
your ways' (NIV).

For silent contemplation, be free to use whichever version speaks most clearly to *you*. I was moved to select
'Consider your way of life' for three reasons: first, because
it makes the clearest and most incisive sense to *me*;
secondly, because it is among the shortest of the various
versions, only five words instead of six or eight; and
thirdly, because, as we shall see, it can be more easily shortened even further. For contemplation, the shorter the phrase
the better.

Before getting down to the work of contemplating this particular Word, it is important, as we have seen, to see it in its biblical context and relationship to the Christian tradition, and to understand it in terms of our own experience.

Old Testament history tells us that in the year 536 BC, the Jews, who had been living in exile in Babylon, were able to return to Palestine. According to the prophet Ezra, the first thing they did was to set up an altar:

> The Israelites now being . . . assembled as one man in Jerusalem . . . Jeshua son of Jozadak and his fellow priests, and Zerubbabel son of Shealtiel and his kinsmen, set to work and built the altar of the God of Israel . . . They put the altar in place first . . .
>
> (Ezra 3:1–3, NEB)

The following year they laid the foundation of the Temple:

> They appointed Levites . . . to supervise the work of the House of the Lord . . . When the builders had laid the foundation of the temple . . . they chanted praises and thanksgiving to the Lord, singing, 'It is good to give thanks to the Lord, for his love . . . endures for ever.'
>
> (Ezra 3:8–11, NEB)

Having laid the foundation, the work of Temple building came to a stop. The site remained a wasteland for a period of fifteen years. The rebuilding work was suspended for two reasons: the Jews refused the co-operation of 'semi-pagans' who had colonised the north of Palestine; and the Jews themselves, perhaps influenced by disillusioned priests, Levites and other leading figures, simply lost interest.

It seems the Jews were primarily and busily engaged in working on their own homes, a self-centred preoccupation which proved to be a recipe for disaster.

Enter Haggai:

> The word of the Lord came through the prophet
> Haggai to Zerubbabel . . . governor of Judah, and to
> Joshua . . . the high priest: These are the words of the
> Lord of hosts: This nation says to itself that it is not yet
> time for the Temple of the Lord to be rebuilt . . . Is it a
> time for you to live in your own well-roofed houses,
> while this Temple lies in ruins? . . . Consider your way
> of life. You have sown much but reaped little; you eat
> but never as much as you wish, you drink but never
> more than you need, you are clothed but never warm,
> and the labourer puts his wages into a purse with a
> hole in it . . . Consider your way of life . . .
>
> (Haggai 1:1–7, NEB)

If you own a Good News Bible, turn to the book of
Haggai. There you will find a simple line drawing which
makes Haggai's point exactly: well-built houses surround-
ing a Temple which is nothing but a ruin. The city and the
nation had lost its soul. The Temple, which was meant to be
the heart, centre, pivot and source of well-being for the
whole city and nation, lay ruined, neglected, ignored.

Consider your way of life . . .

First period of silence

Preparing the heart

Can we see ourselves in any of this? The story of the Jews,
and especially of the Temple, is your story and my story –
the story of every human being who has ever lived or ever
will live. But for the moment, I want to cut a long story
short and get to the point clearly made in the *New*
Testament: *you* are the Temple. St Paul wrote in his letters
to the Christians of Corinth: 'Surely you know that you are
God's temple, where the Spirit of God dwells . . .'
(1 Corinthians 3:16) and 'Don't you know that your body is
the temple of the Holy Spirit . . .?' (2 Corinthians 6:19).
More crucially, St John's Gospel says of Jesus: 'The temple

he was speaking of was his body' (John 2:21, GNB).

You are the Temple, not some special bit of you, but the *whole* of you: the whole thinking, feeling, striving flesh and blood human being which is you.

It is here that the fine, sharp, prophetic Word, spoken through Haggai, cuts in: 'Consider your way of life.'

You may be lucky enough to have a decent roof over your head. You may even have spent a great deal of time, energy, skill and money on house and garden. That does not necessarily lead to a sense of personal (or family) well-being. Evidence suggests that the lives of people who live in this way can often be empty, and in the greatest state of neglect and ruin. I knew, for example, of one married couple in their mid-forties. They had a fine, spacious, beautifully furnished bungalow, an expensive car and river launch. They were deeply in debt, were both drinking heavily, and were constantly violent towards each other. You may not have reached that kind of extreme, but the vital question remains: what kind of a temple are you, at this point in your life?

One thing can be said with certainty: you are not a perfect temple. If you are able even to begin to face the truth, you are bound to recognise in yourself, whatever the reasons may be, something of a sad, sinful and sorry mess: something of a muddled mind, hardened heart and weakened will; something of apathy and disregard of that Divine love which is central, pivotal and the source of well-being for all authentic human living.

Consider your way of life . . .

Second period of silence

Engaging the will

You have now in some measure received this Word from the Divine Source, this challenging command. It does not take much imagination to see how relevant it is to other people and situations in the world at large, whether among your own acquaintances or in the national or international scene. So now is the time for some contemplative intercession. Take a few seconds to re-focus on the Saying, which is being spoken now to your *will*, the active and doing part of your nature . . . 'Consider your way of life'. Now bring into your silence those people or concerns that you have it in mind to pray for. Let the Holy Spirit guide you in this, for it is frequently the case that he will let you know who or what you should be remembering in prayer.

This is where you need to have a kind of twin focus – having in mind the object of your intercession and at the same time remaining in touch with the Saying. The way to do this is first of all to realise that the Saying, which is and conveys the spirit and life of God, is being spoken not just to you, but also to the person or situation you are praying for. Remember how Jesus said, 'My words (i.e., the Word of I AM) which are spirit and life will never pass away' (Mark 13:31; John 6:63, NEB). They are spoken continually, in eternity, to every person and concern in all creation.

Once you understand that, you are authorised by the Lord I AM to speak out the Word in his Name. So instead of asking God to do this or that for John or Mary, you can say silently, and with authority: 'You John; you Mary; consider your way of life.' Or: 'You [this or that person in trouble, or in a position of power and responsibility] . . . consider your way of life.'

This is so much more meaningful than conventional intercession in which you tend to blur the edges of the prayer with your own anxieties, by focusing on the symptoms or problems rather than on the Word of God who knows much better than we do exactly what the real problems are.

Consider your way of life . . .

Thanksgiving

At the end of the allotted time for your contemplative prayer and intercession, don't forget to say thank you to God for the riches of his blessing which have been received by you and those for whom you have prayed, and re-dedicate your life in his service. You can use the prayer in the Notes (p.123), or one of your own.

9   Your spiritual inheritance

Preliminary

First of all we spend two minutes silently listening to the Divine Invitation: 'Come unto ME all you who labour and are heavy laden, and I will give you rest' (Matthew 11:28, AV).

You are my beloved (Son) . . . I AM (your) inheritance.

> (Mark 1:11, REB and Numbers 18:20, AV.
> See also Matthew 3:7)

Preparing the mind

The first part of the commentary is to prepare our *minds* to hear and receive the Word of God spoken in scripture. The feast of the Epiphany (6 January in the Church's Calendar) is associated primarily with the visit of the Magi to the Christ-child, but in the passage of 'sacred time' (which is the Church's liturgical year beginning in Advent) the season of the Epiphany is also linked with the baptism of Jesus by John the Baptist at the river Jordan, as this verse from a fifth-century Epiphany hymn indicates:

> *The Lamb of God is manifest*
> *again in Jordan's water blest,*
> *and he who sin had never known*
> *by washing hath our sins undone.*
>
> (English Hymnal 38, 1933 ed.)

Like our own baptism, this event is of crucial importance; it is a re-generation, an affirmation of sacred identity, as much for Jesus by the river as for us when we were given a Christian name at the font. The voice of God sets the seal on this highly-charged event. 'You are MY beloved Son in whom I am well pleased.' The voice is for our sake as well as his. We, too, are God's beloved children, and Jesus drew his disciples' attention to the importance of that relationship in his teaching on prayer: 'When you pray, say, "Father . . ." ' (Luke 11:2, REB; see also Matthew 6: 6–9).

The question of identity was a very important one for the Jews, and still is. It is naturally important for us as well, but we tend to think of identity in terms of the individual, whereas for the Jews it was a question also of race, culture and spiritual significance; which is why we have those long genealogies in the Bible. This sense of corporate identity also lends significance to the location of Jesus' baptism. For John was calling the nation to spiritual renewal by repentance at the precise point where Joshua had crossed the river Jordan to enter the Promised Land. So here, at the point of entry, comes the call and challenge to a new beginning, and we, by baptism, are inheritors of that situation, continually called to make a new start and encourage others to do the same.

Closely tied in with the question of identity is the question of inheritance. It is for this reason that I have made a composite Saying from two different parts of the Bible, by using the words from the book of Numbers 'I AM your inheritance' to round the Saying off. Interestingly, the old Prayer Book catechism underlines this connection, beginning with the two questions:

Q. What is your name?
A. [Name . . .]
Q. Who gave you that name?
A. My Godfathers and Godmothers in my Baptism, wherein I was made a member of Christ, a child of God, and an *inheritor* of the kingdom of heaven.

In traditional Jewish law, those who were enrolled in the sacred service of the sanctuary, the Aaronic priests and the

Levites, had to forfeit their earthly inheritance and live on tithed offerings. This was because they had to recognise that I AM was their inheritance (Deuteronomy 10:9; Joshua 13:33. See also Psalm 16:5). Because we share in the royal priesthood of Christ (see 1 Peter 2:9 and Revelation 1:6), whatever our earthly status, our true inheritance is spiritual, 'kept for us in heaven' – a concept which St Paul liked to teach (Romans 8:17; Galatians 3:29; Ephesians 3:6).

As gender is irrelevant in God's kingdom, we can legitimately remove the word 'Son' as we listen to this Saying spoken to our minds from the Divine Source.

You are MY beloved . . . I AM your inheritance . . .

First period of silence

Preparing the heart

The second part of the commentary will prepare us to receive this Word more deeply within us, in our *heart.* Let us remember how it is a word of affirmation, not just of our spiritual nature, but of our full humanity. The words that Jesus heard were, 'You are MY beloved Son; in you I take delight' ('in whom I am well pleased'). Jesus accepts this without demur, and by his ministry to both body and soul (healing and self-oblation) he, who was fully human as well as divine, gave to our religion its distinctively incarnational character.

But the primacy is with the spiritual, which means that we are called not to exalt the material but to keep it firmly in its place. I understand that, in Malawi, inheritance passes from uncle to nephew rather than from father to son. I met a Malawian priest some years ago who had a wealthy uncle – unusual in a country so poor. The family was Muslim. When as a young man the priest converted to Christianity, the family was predictably angry. Matters became worse when he said he was offering himself for ordination, and his uncle tried to win him back by saying that if he re-converted his inheritance would be secure, but otherwise he would be disinherited. It cannot have been easy for this young man, aligning himself to one of the poorest Anglican churches in our communion, to have asserted with simple courage, 'God is my inheritance.'

Our founder, Robert Coulson, was himself born into a wealthy upper class family in Russia. They had very considerable holdings in Estonia, which was then part of the Russian empire. As the eldest son, Robert was heir to this vast inheritance. But they lost the lot in the Revolution of 1917 and barely escaped to England with their lives. In subsequent years, after obeying his calling to priesthood and the contemplative life, he said more than once, and with complete candour, 'The loss of that inheritance was the best thing that could have happened to me!'[1]

We listen now to this Saying spoken to us in our hearts, gently focusing on the words by mental repetition to the exclusion of other thoughts.

You are MY beloved . . . I AM your inheritance . . .

Second period of silence

Engaging the will

In intercession, there should be no difficulty in seeing how this Saying is relevant to many human situations, and we might also remember those who bear responsibility for the world's wealth – financiers, bankers, lawyers etc.

Another important way in which the will is engaged as a result of contemplative prayer is the use of the Saying as a Watchword in daily life. You should try to remain mindful of the Saying at times other than just prayer time. The chances are that you will be too busily engaged during the day about your various tasks at work or elsewhere. But now and again it is not difficult to recall momentarily the Saying, or part of it. Sometimes there may be a special point in doing so. For instance, if you are experiencing some anxiety, or if for some reason your self-esteem is low, the words 'You are MY beloved' can be a very effective Watchword. It will remind you of your true status in the realm of the spirit. If you are concerned about money, especially about the lack of it, the Word 'I AM your inheritance' will serve as a constant and necessary reminder not to rely on the illusion of material wealth, and to realise the true source of all wealth and security.

You are MY beloved . . . I AM your inheritance . . .

Thanksgiving

End with a prayer of thanksgiving for God's 'unsearchable riches' and offer yourself afresh in the service of our Lord, I AM.

10

My resting place, my home, my desire

Preliminary

Take just two minutes listening to the Lord saying to you:
'Come unto ME, all you who labour and are heavy laden,
and I will give you rest.' If there is a particular burden, care
or anxiety that you are carrying, this is the time to lay it
down at the foot of the cross of Christ.

> **This is my resting-place for ever; here will I make
> my home, for such is my desire.** (Psalm 132:14, NEB)

Preparing the mind

This verse of the Psalms refers to the Temple which stood
at the heart of Jerusalem. The words, which are attributed
to God, may have been chanted by a Temple priest or cultic
prophet.

The Psalms have been regarded and used for many
centuries in both the Hebrew and Christian traditions as an
anthology of religious poems. In several places, they give
valuable insights into the way a devout Jew viewed the
Temple, the way he addressed himself to the God who had
made his home there:

> *O Lord, I love the beauty of thy house*
> *the place where thy glory dwells.*
>
> *Holiness is the beauty of thy temple.*
>
> *Happy is the man of thy choice, whom thou dost bring to*
> *dwell in thy courts;*

let us enjoy the blessing of thy house,
thy holy temple.

I, through thy great love, may come into thy house,
and bow low toward thy holy temple in awe of thee.

I will bring sacrifices into thy temple
and fulfil my vows to thee.

[People] are filled with the rich plenty of thy house,
and thou givest them water from the flowing stream of thy
delights;
for with thee is the fountain of life
and in thy light we are bathed with light.

Even the sparrow finds a home,
and the swallow has her nest,
where she rears her brood beside thy altars . . .
Happy are those who dwell in thy house;
they never cease from praising thee.

O God, we re-enact the story of thy true love
within thy temple;
the praise thy name deserves, O God,
is heard at earth's farthest bounds. [1]

I cannot help but see the Lord taking hold of those words and changing them into an expression of his own essential nature. Through those words from the Psalms I hear him speaking directly, clearly – not to the Temple in Jerusalem, but to you and me personally, because '*You* are the Temple':

You are the Temple. I love the beauty of you, the place where my glory dwells. Holiness is the beauty of my Temple. Happy the people I choose, whom I bring to dwell in you; let them enjoy the blessing of my house, my holy Temple. They, through my great love, may come into you and bow low towards you in awe of me. They will bring sacrifices into you and fulfil their vows unto me. People are filled with the rich plenty they find in you, and I give them water from the flowing stream of my delights; for with me is the fountain of life, and in my light they are bathed with light.

Even the animal world finds a home in you. Happy

are those who dwell in you; they never cease from
praising me. They re-enact the story of my true love
within you, my Temple; the praise my name deserves
is heard at earth's farthest bounds.[1]

This poses many intriguing and challenging questions.
However, whatever the questions, there is no doubt that it
represents a powerful, positive, affirmative view of your
humanity. You are the Temple, loved, beautiful, glorious,
holy, enabling people to find happiness, blessing, and
humility before the awesomeness of God; and all the rest!

Every single key word and image deserves unwrapping
and pursuing. For the moment, I select only the first of them:
love.

'I love the beauty of you,' says God. 'People, through my
great love, may come into you.'

The witness of the Scriptures and of the contemplative
tradition, is that God burns with love for you and all
humankind – that his love is a strong, tender, compassionate love[2], that he longs for you to 'Make your home in
me, as I make mine in you' (John 15:3, JB), that he aches for
you to hear and receive and live by the Word that comes
from his mouth: '[You are] my resting-place for ever; [in
you] I will make my home, for such is my desire.'

Your struggle to build yourself into a Temple to the glory
of God, in which God can rest and make a home, is itself
your loving response to God's great love for you.

> **This is my resting-place for ever; here will I make
> my home, for such is my desire . . .**

First period of silence

Preparing the heart

It is worth remembering how on occasions God's love
burns with passion and anger, because of the un-holiness
of his human creation. There is no need to give examples:
just turn a few pages of the Bible at random among the

books of the prophets and you will see what I mean. Jesus, too, expresses anger; most notably against the people who insist on turning the Temple of God into a market place (John 3:12–17).

We tend to think of anger as a destructive force, which, if uncontrolled, it can be. But it may also be used creatively, and that creative anger is an essential ingredient of God's love and of all authentic human love. If you have begun to catch a glimpse of the kind of Temple you were created to be, then in the light of that vision you will become aware of how that Temple, which should be holy, has become damaged through neglect. Then you, too, may share with God something of his angry frustration.

As we have seen, this Word of God was probably proclaimed through a priest or prophet, to those who came to worship in the Temple at Jerusalem: 'This is my resting-place for ever; here I will make my home, for such is my desire.' Because, in Christian terms '*You* are the Temple', these words can also be heard addressed personally to you and to every aspect of your human nature.

We all have hidden depths, levels of consciousness about which we know very little, lurking within our psyche. They may come close to the surface in our dreams, and may affect the way we behave, especially when we are emotionally upset. Yet these subconscious or unconscious levels of our personality are indeed mysterious and often impenetrable. Yet they are part of our created nature, and therefore they must be known by God. And if known by him, they must also be loved by him and available, if need be, to his healing touch through the penetrative power of his Word.

Within the Jerusalem Temple, right at the centre, was the Holy Place, hidden from the view of everyone except for the High Priest who was allowed to enter it just once each year. Our hidden psychological depths contain such a Holy Place . . . 'My resting-place for ever.'

The clearer this truth becomes to you – the more it

becomes 'heart knowledge' – the clearer you will see that this word is for you. And not for you alone, but for *every* human being, for every last scrap of this and every planet, and for the vastness of space in which they are set: You, everyone and everything is MY Temple, loved, beautiful, glorious, holy, in which to find happiness, blessing, a humble awareness of Me, and all the rest.

This reminds me of the visionary language of Meister Eckhart:

> You must understand that all creatures are by nature endeavouring to be like God. The heavens would not revolve unless they followed on the track of God or of his likeness. If God were not in all things, nature would stop dead, not working and not wanting, for whether you like it or not, whether you know it or not, nature fundamentally is seeking . . . and tending towards God . . . Nature . . . seeks and ever more hotly . . . pursues the trail of God. [3]

If you have grasped something of this poetic truth, you are bound to be impelled to do the work of thanksgiving and intercession — to allow God to channel his Word through you — to let yourself be caught up in his desire for the well-being of everyone and everything — to share his joy, praise, even ecstasy over all the lovely and glorious holy Temple building that is going on in people and in the whole creation. You can become, through intercession, a channel of the Word to all this, sharing its spirit and life, releasing the laughter and tears which come with the recognition that the Word *is* being fulfilled in countless people and places which are, 'My resting-place . . . My home . . . My desire.'

But first you must receive this Saying into that deeper, hidden, emotional part of your being, into you heart.

This is my resting-place for ever; here will I make my home, for such is my desire . . .

Second period of silence

Engaging the will

You will probably find it easier to shorten the Saying for intercession and for use as a Watchword. Try simply, 'My resting-place; My home; My desire'. I have shown how this Word from the Lord is relevant for all creation, but in intercession you may find it particularly relevant for the Church, its leaders and members, and for faithful people of other religious persuasions.

In daily life, this Watchword can be a great help if you, or anyone you meet or have to deal with, are for some reason disturbed emotionally, feeling lost or unloved. Grasp this Saying as a 'sword of the spirit' to remind you of the abiding presence of God who is our eternal home.

My resting-place . . . my home . . . my desire . . .

Thanksgiving

End the exercise with the customary prayer of thanksgiving and rededication.

11

Be still; know God

Preliminary

Listen for just two minutes to the Divine Invitation: 'Come unto ME, all you who labour and are heavy laden, and I will give you rest.' It applies to you, of course, but also to anyone about whom you may be anxious. So, if you feel burdened on account of someone else's trouble, then lay that, too, at the feet of the Lord.

Be still and know that I AM God . . .   (Psalm 46:10, AV)

Preparing the mind

In Sally Beauman's novel *Rebecca's Tale*, Rebecca said of her husband: 'Max always wants words to be shackled, so 'love' means this and 'hate' means that; lock them up in a poor prison of sense and slam the door on them . . . I don't agree. Words should take you on journeys.' How aptly this describes the words of scripture, the Word of God. Look merely at the surface meaning of Dominical Sayings and you won't get very far. Listen to them contemplatively, and they will indeed take you on journeys as their spirit and life begin to sink into your inner being.

Be still and know that I AM God. Every single word in this familiar Saying, a favourite among contemplatives, can take you on a journey. 'Be' . . . now is the time for *being* rather than *doing*. It was said of one bustling Christian lady: 'She was forever doing good to other people; and you could tell who the 'other people' were by the hunted look on their faces.' In the eighteenth century, Jonathan Swift once said, 'Some (people) are so busy about their religion that they hardly have time to say their prayers.' The good life, that is, the life of goodness, will be a true balance between being and doing.

'Be still'. True stillness, like silence, is a rare and precious commodity in our hyperactive and noisy world. Our characteristic restlessness is a real symptom of God-less-ness, and the fruit of that is stress, which is one of the greatest causes of sickness and malaise in Western society. Even in times of so-called relaxation, unless we are asleep, the radio and TV are twittering and flickering with restlessness. How vital it is for us to pay attention to God calling us, in the middle of all this cacophony, to 'be still'.

'And know'. Even the little word 'and' is significant here. Having taken time out simply to *be*, having achieved at least some measure of stillness and recognition of the Lord's command, the word 'and' tells you that something important is about to take place in your life. There is to be a 'knowing'. Not just a new piece of information made available to your already teeming brain, but a real biblical 'knowing' which speaks of a deepening of spiritual understanding and relationship, an insight into the mystery of God, whose truest name is I AM. 'I AM' is the holy revelation of Divine Truth given to Moses at the burning bush (Exodus 3:14). Space does not allow any further thoughts on this profound Saying; but anyway, now is the time for listening rather than for thinking.

Be still, and know that I AM God . . .

First period of silence

Preparing the heart

You might say, using traditional folk language, that the devil is actively engaged in preventing people from praying. However you think of it, there appears to be a malign opposition at work each time we attempt to deepen our prayer-relationship with God. Sometimes this is within the subtle depths of your own being, a weariness and heavy disinclination to pray, and a feeling that you would be better employed doing something else, almost anything else.

Sometimes, on the other hand, it is an open and quite unsubtle attack. I have been on dozens of retreats, most of them in idyllic places of peace and quiet. I cannot tell you how many times, when we have settled down to silent prayer, that the rural calm of the retreat house has been fractured by someone deciding, at that very moment, to mow the grass, or clean the windows, or start up a tractor in a nearby field, or get some flying practice in at the local airport, or repair an outhouse with saw and hammer or, on one occasion, mend just that bit of remote country road alongside the house.

Perhaps the devil is taking exception because more people are seeking peace and true rest. Certainly a greater number are now realising the value of retreats and the need for stillness and quiet. So maybe this is reason why 'the opposition' is overtly more active in trying to put a stop to it, and to prevent that deepening of the spiritual life which leads us toward our God and our salvation.

I was tempted more than once to give in and do something else. Then I received a clear sign that the devil could not win if I was truly seeking inner stillness and the peace of God. I was visiting the Dorothy Kerin home of healing at Burrswood in Surrey and I went into the chapel for half an hour of contemplative prayer. It was a lovely sunny afternoon and the chapel was calm and peaceful and, I thought, empty. After three minutes the deep silence was completely shattered by an horrific clatter. A workman, unseen round a corner, had started to use a masonry drill to erect some fitting on one of the walls.

My first reaction was to get up and go. But suddenly I was told, inwardly but in no uncertain terms, that it wouldn't do to let 'the opposition' get away with it. So I sat down again, regained my composure and re-focused on this Saying from Psalm 46: *Be still and know that I AM God.*

The workman continued drilling intermittently during the rest of that half-hour. But to my utter amazement, I spent one of the most truly peace-full times that I have ever experienced. If I wanted a sign, I couldn't have had a clearer one. Ever since then, it has been much easier to deal with 'the opposition', and even to treat the devil with the contempt he deserves, knowing that, by the grace of God, contemplatives are on the winning side.

Be still and know that I AM God . . .

Second period of silence

Engaging the will

Some people like to write the Saying that they are currently using in contemplative prayer on a small card which they then keep in a pocket or handbag. It can be a reminder at odd times during the day. This particular Saying is very helpful when, for whatever reason, life seems to be more fraught or frustrating than usual. For intercession, there is no lack of people or situations in varying states of un-stillness for whom this Word from the Lord will be particularly relevant.

Be still, and know that I AM God . . .

Thanksgiving

Prayer of thanksgiving and rededication.

12

Your boundaries

Preliminary

As usual, spend just two minutes in relaxed and alert silence, listening to the Lord's invitation: 'Come unto ME, all you who labour and are heavy laden, and I will give you rest.' This 'rest' is not mere leisure time. The Greek word is *anapausis*, literally a creative 'pause' in the concerns of everyday life, for re-freshment.

> **All your boundary stones shall be jewels . . .**
> (Isaiah 54:12, NEB)

Preparing the mind

A poet once said, 'Humankind cannot bear very much reality' (T. S. Eliot). Another, 'The world is too much with us' (Wordsworth). Karl Marx famously described religion as an opiate for the masses. He lived and taught at a time when the scientific outlook was gaining ground and people were focusing more and more on the material and physical world. In the nineteenth century, intelligent people increasingly were of the opinion that there was no reality beyond what could be seen and felt, measured and analysed.

A good deal of measurable and experiential reality in Karl Marx's day was the squalor and poverty to be found in the burgeoning of industry in the developing nations of the Western world. This erupted in the horror of the technological wars of the twentieth century and rumbles on in the economic imbalances in the world of the twenty-first century. Still, in our own day, a considerable proportion of thinking human beings fail to grasp that there could be any kind of reality beyond the worldly.

For them, a great deal of scripture must be quite incomprehensible and meaningless, because it tells of an unknowable God, of a life of the spirit, of visions of perfection in heaven and of a kingdom not of this world. The Bible does not dodge real issues which affect humanity, nor does it side-step the mundane concerns of people and their day-to-day problems. Often the biblical scene is dark and familiar, with conflict and violence, greed and selfishness, deprivation and disaster both natural and man-made.

Yet all the way through, the biblical record is shot through with beams of light and flashes of hope. And undergirding all is the knowledge of a sub-structure, or super-structure, of spiritual reality of which this world and universe are, materially speaking, mere fragments.

When they talk of this spiritual reality, the biblical writers, prophets and others, have recourse to the language of poetry, and their vision is expressed in terms of myth, symbol and imagery as they respond to what they know and experience of reality from God's point of view.

In particular, this is noticeable at the beginning and the end of the Bible. Genesis 1 and 2, and Revelation 21 and 22, stand like divine quotation marks at the start and the conclusion of the created order. Their focus is not on squalor and sinfulness, but on perfection and glory. The fulfilment of God's good and loving purposes, spelt out in the goodness of creation 'in the beginning', is seen in the splendour of the New Jerusalem at the end of time. In stunning contrast to the Jerusalem as we know it today, the city of God is made of jewels, resplendent in beauty and perfect in design.

This is not mere poetic fancy, but a visionary and prophetic utterance of the destiny of God's creation. Isaiah had a personal experience of God's glory (Isaiah 6:1–8), and his message is a stimulus to God's people to work within and for that glory, and never to lose sight of the vision of perfection, symbolised by the restored Jerusalem built of jewels, bright and beautiful.

All your boundary stones shall be Jewels . . .

First period of silence

Preparing the heart

I believe that this Saying has a strong personal strand woven into it. When we understand this, we shall find the Saying to be meaningful for us at a deeper level, the heart-level, and it will make good sense in our intercessions.

In the Bible, the symbolism of precious stones is not just related to architecture, but is also more closely connected with people. In Exodus 28, you will find those same jewels, of which the Holy City is built in Revelation, mentioned as part of the high-priestly vestments of Aaron. We must admit that we cannot now fully penetrate the mystic significance of this, but we can respond to something of the psychology of beauty and value relating to us as persons. It is also spiritually important for us to see ourselves as precious and valued, both with respect to other people and in the sight of God (Isaiah 43:4. See also 1 Peter 2:4–7 where the valued stones are the foundations of God's spiritual 'city' composed of faith-full people).

We all have our personal 'walls', or 'boundary stones' – the translations of this Saying differ but the significance of the Word is not much changed. It has been said, 'good fences make good neighbours'. Boundaries are important; they help us to be secure in our identity. We sometimes talk about our private space, and say that we don't like it when other people invade it.

Boundaries are also our front to the world. Flags often fly at boundaries; they are the places where we show our colours. However important they may be, boundaries can also easily become a huge problem. This is obvious on the international scale. But personally, if we are insecure or feel threatened, then we start, metaphorically speaking, to put up shutters or build higher walls and fences. Then we hide behind these defences (psychologists talk about 'defence mechanisms') and either we become aggressive, throwing missiles at the world outside, or we retreat into our shell (another boundary metaphor) of personal misery.

So this Word from the Lord can be both timely and health-giving. He will not demolish our boundaries, for God does not violate the freedom that he has given us. But it is in his power, with our co-operation, to transform our boundaries into precious stones, changing a desolate no-man's-land into an item of beauty and value. Once this transformation begins to occur, then relationships can be built, trust can be established, and reconciliation can happen.

By God's grace, this is actually happening among human beings all the time, in spite of what the media may tell us to the contrary. It is the prophet's vision that God is building his kingdom in this way, and that ultimately, the glory of this process will prevail universally, when God is all in all. Then, not only shall we see the Holy City in its resplendent, be-jewelled magnificence, but we shall ourselves be part of it.

All your boundary stones shall be jewels . . .

Second period of silence

Engaging the will

You can use this Saying to great effect as a 'Watchword'. A Watchword is a calling to mind at odd moments (especially first thing in the morning and last thing at night) of the Saying that has been used in contemplative prayer. We all have times when we feel wretched and undervalued, perhaps because we have failed when others have apparently succeeded. These words from the Lord remind us how, in his sight, we are always both loved and precious.

And as we intercede for those less fortunate than ourselves, perhaps in desperate straits, we can, in the spirit, offer them this assurance that, whatever the world may think, God thinks of all his human creation as jewels of infinite value.

All your boundary stones shall be jewels . . .

Thanksgiving

Say your prayer of thanksgiving and rededication in the service of God.

13 Resurrection and life

Preliminary

We take our customary two minutes to listen in silence to
God's invitation to pay close attention to what he has to
say: 'Come unto ME all you who labour and are heavy
laden, and I will give you rest' (Matthew 11:28, AV).

I AM the Resurrection and the Life ...   (John 11:25)

Preparing the mind

For the first five of these six contemplative exercises, we
have selected most of the Sayings from the Old Testament.
This will help and reassure those Christians who may
consider that 'their' Bible is the New Testament. Remember,
however, that the first Christians had only the Jewish
scriptures, and recognised in *them* the revelation of God
through his Word.

However, I have chosen as our final Word that supreme
'I AM' Saying from St John's Gospel which acts as a kind of
theological capstone to the great spiritual edifice of the
scriptures of both testaments.

In general, the Old Testament is fairly gloomy about
death and its aftermath. As people die, they are described
vaguely as 'sleeping with their ancestors' (see, for example,
2 Kings 20:21) in some impenetrable limbo. We are 'like the
beasts that perish', and our death is a 'descent into the Pit',
a sort of grey non-life where 'no man remembereth thee'
(see various Psalms, for example, Psalm 88). That little shaft

of sunlight in the book of Job, 'I know that my redeemer liveth' (Job 19:25, AV), only serves to show up the general air of darkness which surrounds the whole of the Old Testament attitude to dying and death.

During the 200–300 years before the birth of Jesus, the Jewish people had to submit to a good deal of oppression and persecution from foreign rulers. During this time, it began to be felt that a just and loving God could not simply condemn either innocent victims or brave warriors who died in the cause of freedom to total annihilation, or even to an endless shadowy existence deep beneath the flat earth. Ideas of resurrection came to the fore at this time, and in Jesus' day there were quite fierce debates going on about these doctrines, some of which are reflected in the gospel record (Matthew 22:23 ff.). The teachings were often quite crudely materialistic (Matthew 27:52–53), and even to this day many Jews want to be buried as close as possible to the site of the old temple, so that, on the day of resurrection, they will be among the first to enter the gate of the new Jerusalem. Martha's conversation with Jesus is based on this discussion in first century Judaism, as is some of St Paul's teaching on the resurrection in 1 Corinthians 15.

The first Christians shared these views to some extent, and the accounts of the resurrection of Jesus are very physical, focusing on the tomb and his material presence among his followers. This Saying 'I AM the Resurrection and the Life' is inviting us to broaden our vision and embrace more widely the loving purposes of God seen in Jesus, as Lord of life and death. Jesus here uses the great words 'I AM' (in Greek, *eimai*), which is the mysterious and sacred Name of God revealed to Moses (Exodus 3:14). As a result, suddenly, in this Saying, the whole enigma of death is illuminated with glory and hope. However grim and foreboding are the human experiences relating to death and dissolution, the Lord is sovereign of all. Our problems are not magically resolved, but by aligning ourselves in faith with the death and resurrection of Christ, we can share in the promise of eternal life and glimpse the glory that is still to be revealed (1 John 3:2).

I AM the Resurrection and the Life . . .

First period of silence

Preparing the heart

As we contemplate this Word of the Lord, we are certainly caught up in realms of the mystery of God who is above and beyond all that we can comprehend. Yet God is also 'through all and in all' (Ephesians 4:6, AV). We recall that this Saying was spoken in the physical context of sheer human grief at the loss of a dear brother. In John Chapter 11 we are at the home of Mary and Martha and Lazarus, good friends of Jesus, who lived at Bethany near Jerusalem.

We do not need much imagination to enter this story – to feel as they felt in their sorrow and bereavement. At the same time, we have the advantage of being on the other side of the cross and resurrection of Jesus. We have, as it were, a powerful ally when we find ourselves having to face suffering and death. We can grasp this 'sword of the Spirit' from John 11:25, and we can understand even better than Martha something of the vast significance of this Saying – something of the vital 'spirit and life' which the words convey.

Beyond whatever comfort we can personally gather from this Saying when we suffer or grieve, I like to recall how these words constitute and summarise one of the greatest of the treasures that the Christian faith has to offer to the world. Whenever I am called, following a death, to visit a house where there are grieving relatives or friends, before I ring the doorbell, I make the sign of the cross with my thumb on the wall or doorpost, and call to mind this Saying, 'I AM the Resurrection and the Life.' This simple action means that, during the visit, whether the family are aware of it or not, the whole household is spiritually enfolded within God's love and the Christian hope in eternal life through the death and resurrection of Jesus.

Our generation has, by and large, parted company with a living faith in God. Consequently it has lost its way and is drifting like an anchorless ship on an ocean of doubt, and sometimes of despair when it comes to coping with dying, death and the hereafter. People are often desperately in need of the firm and confident faith of those of us who not only believe in 'the Resurrection and the Life', but live by that faith which can banish our fear of dying and death.

As we receive this Saying, not simply intellectually, but more profoundly within our being in contemplation, we shall both experience something of the fullness of God's love in Jesus, and we shall also be enabled to help others at a time of great need.

I AM the Resurrection and the Life . . .

Second period of silence

Engaging the will

My little habitual action described above at the door of a bereaved household is one way of putting the Word of God to work in a fairly common situation. Also, you can bring this Saying to mind whenever you attend a funeral or memorial service, or when you come across stories of untimely or violent death as you watch or read the news. In this way you will bring spiritual help to those in need at a time when, for them, God may seem far away. And, of course, use the Saying in intercession for those who grieve, especially for people with little or no faith, as well as for your own dead relatives and friends.

I AM the Resurrection and the Life . . .

Thanksgiving

Prayer of thanksgiving and rededication.

Part
3

Conclusion

We need to recognise that the contemplative way of prayer and life also includes a strong commitment to a local congregation, commitment to its worship and prayer, fellowship and care, witness and mission. I realise that this thought may be uncomfortable for some, but it is nevertheless true. You should be able to take your experience of silence into the life of your church, and, with appropriate tact and discretion, share what you have found with the clergy, with other leaders, and with the people. Like the healed man in Luke 8, tell them what God has done for you. Keep them all regularly in your silent prayer.

It is encouraging that many churches are now finding opportunities for times of quiet, sometimes with days away, sometimes during the course of the worship itself. The Church of England prayer book, *Common Worship,* specifically mentions the inclusion of times of silence during the service. Many churchgoers are mystified about what to do in those quiet times. You may have a vital ministry to offer here; a ministry of enabling others silently to hear and receive the Word, and to live by the Word.

Some of what you share is bound to fall, like the seed in the parable, on stony ground, but some will fall on good soil and bear abundant fruit. Perhaps, one day, all the churches, and other religious congregations as well, will discover their desperate need to 'Be silent before ME', to 'Be attentive to every word of MINE', so that every word will 'accomplish MY purpose'.

When the churches and congregations can be *seen* to be

doing this, there will be some hope for the world, even for the world of politics which needs to discover the truth of Charles Péguy's dictum that 'everything begins in mysticism (i.e. in the mind, heart and will of God) and ends in politics'. We shall then have an authentic kind of politics which has at heart the true well-being of all humanity and the rest of the animal, vegetable and mineral creation. This will be a kind of politics which enables the kingdom, or rule, of God to have supreme sovereignty over every human being and institution, a kind of politics that is wide open to and motivated by the Word.

You will sometimes find in silent prayer that your contemplative exercise will throw into sharp and painful focus just how far removed from 'truth' our current political attitudes and policies are. How tragic it is that so many policies are literally the lesser of two *evils*. Our contemplative 'work' is vital to bring spiritual influence to bear in such situations, and to support the people who often have to make desperate choices.

We will let Jan van Ruysbroeck, the fourteenth-century Flemish theologian and mystic, have the last word:

> A person who has been sent [from contemplation] into the world is full of truth and rich in all virtues. He seeks nothing of his own but only the glory of the One who sent him. He is accordingly righteous and truthful in all things and has a rich and generous foundation which rests on God's own richness. He will therefore always flow forth to all who need him, for the living spring of the Holy Spirit is so rich that it can never be drained dry. Such a person is a living and willing instrument of God with which God accomplishes what he *wishes in the way he wishes . . . May God grant that we all attain this. Amen.*
>
> (From his book *The Spiritual Espousals and other Works*)

Appendix

The Fellowship of Contemplative Prayer (FCP)

At the time of the publication of this book, the principal contacts for the Fellowship are the Administrator and the Chaplain.

Administrator
Mrs Margaret Hall
9 All Saints Close, Asfordby, Melton Mowbray
Leicestershire LE14 3TF
mj.hall100@virgin.net

Chaplain
The Revd. Canon Charles Dobbin
St John's Rectory, Fir Tree Lane
Leeds, Yorkshire LS17 7BZ

The FCP Website can be found at:
www.contemplative-prayer.org.uk.

There are members and groups in the United Kingdom, Ireland, US, South Africa and Australia (West and East). Members are bound together by a simple Rule (see *Adopting a Rule of Life* in Chapter 4). Free explanatory leaflets are available. The Annual Newsletter is also free of charge and contains details of local FCP contacts and a list of annual retreats held in the UK.

The Fellowship is a registered UK charity (298850) with five trustees. It is administered by a Council consisting of the Trustees and three other members. Apart from a few members who have been given life membership, all other members are expected to renew their membership every twelve months if they wish to continue as members.

All FCP groups, quiet days and retreats are open to non-members who may attend with no obligation to join. The Fellowship comprises Christians of all denominations and is welcoming to people of any faith.

The FCP is not affiliated to any other organisation, but most members belong to a church or worshipping congregation. Some are also members of other organisations which encourage the prayer of stillness and silence.

Religious Communities

In Chapter 4 it was suggested that those who attempt to follow the contemplative way should consider being in touch with a religious community. These are too numerous to list here, and you are advised to consult the *UK Christian Handbook* in your local church or library. This is a comprehensive compendium of information relating to a very wide spectrum of Christian activity. Details about the book are available from the publishers Harper Collins (Religious) at 77–85 Fulham Palace Road, London W6 8JB, and the Website www.ukchristianhandbook.org.uk. Details of religious communities in other countries should be available from local churches.

Further reading and other resources

In addition to the free leaflets, the Fellowship of Contemplative Prayer keeps a small stock of books by the founder, Robert G. Coulson, and has produced (to date) eight cassettes containing contemplative exercises. Most of these have been recorded 'live' at FCP retreats by experienced Witnesses of the Word of God. They can be used privately and are suitable for prayer groups. For details please write to the FCP Literature Distribution Secretary (see below).

Some helpful books are mentioned in the Notes below. If you are interested in further reading, by far the best course is to subscribe to the Fellowship's occasional journal *Living Word*. Eight issues have been published to date (2005) and further issues are planned. Each issue contains articles relating to contemplative prayer, and many of the articles consist of extracts from books which FCP members have found helpful and inspiring. Commentaries accompany the extracts to give further assistance in understanding the importance and relevance of the work in question.

By its nature, this journal does not date. Its intention is to build up a useful (and affordable) background resource for contemplation and, as far as possible, to keep in touch with the best of what has been written, and is currently being written, about prayer. The first six issues are priced at £2.45 and issues seven and eight at £3.00 (the price includes postage for single copies, 2005 prices). A good stock of all issues from No.1 onward is kept. They are available from FCP Literature Distribution Secretary:

Mrs Carol Binnie
1 Bachelors Cottage, Long Reach, Ockham, Woking
Surrey GU23 6PG

The Bible

There are now many new translations of the Bible but do not undervalue the Authorised (or King James) Version. It often provides a text that suits contemplative prayer better than modern English. It is always as well to compare different translations, but make sure you use an authentic translation rather than an interpretative text such as *The Living Bible*. Witnesses of the Word will probably want to make use of a good concordance. If you are thinking of buying one, it would be as well to seek advice from your local minister, or look in the reference section of a good library. If you have a computer, enquire about biblical material that is now available on CD-ROM. The New Revised Standard Version Cross-Reference edition (Oxford University Press 2003) is an invaluable resource for any serious Bible reader, especially for Witnesses of the Word.

Notes

Chapter 1

1 Thomas Merton.
2 Clifton Wolters. Introduction to his 1961 Penguin Classics edition of *The Cloud of Unknowing*, p.36.
3 Simone Weil, *Waiting on God* (Fontana, 1959), chapter on 'Reflections on the Right Use of School Studies with a View to the Love of God'.
4 Monica Furlong, *Contemplating Now* (Hodder & Stoughton, 1971), p.13.
5 *Struggle and Contemplation* (Mowbray, 1983) is the title of a book by Brother Roger, Prior of Taizé until 2005. He writes: 'The Christian, even though he be plunged into God's silence, senses an underlying truth: [the] struggle for and with others finds its source in another struggle that is more and more etched in his deepest self . . . There he touches the gates of contemplation' (p.1).
6 Herbert Slade, *Exploration into Contemplative Prayer* (DLT, 1975), p.106.
7 Théodor Bovet, *Have Time and be Free* (SPCK, 1965), p.33
8 John V. Taylor, *The Go-Between God* (SCM Press, 1974) p.237.
9 *The Cloud of Unknowing*, Chapter 4.

Chapter 2

1 The Balts in Estonia were a land-owning aristocracy (distinct from the native Estonians) who were the real 'rulers' of the province until the 1917 revolution. They were of German origin, tracing their ancestry back to the

Teutonic Crusaders known as the Livonian Knights, who originally came from Prussia and became the undisputed masters of the East Baltic region from the thirteenth to the fifteenth centuries.

2 *Spirit and Life*, the biography of R. G. Coulson by Martin Tunnicliffe, was published in 1988 by Churchman Publishing Ltd (the date of publication is 1987 in the book itself, but this is an error). The book came out during Robert Coulson's lifetime. In addition to having a close personal acquaintance with his subject, the author was able to meet with Robert's sister and brother, and with both his daughters, all of whom provided insights into his character. The quotations in this chapter (apart from the final one) are taken from the book. A revised and updated edition of this biography is awaiting publication.

3 Quoted from *Postscript: an anthology of spiritual guidance from the letters of Robert Coulson* (selected and edited by Martin Tunnicliffe, FCP, 1994).

Chapter 3

1 Anthony Hoekema's *Created in God's Image* (Paternoster Press, 1986) is a good exploration of the subject.

2 [All quotations are from the *Revised English Bible* unless otherwise indicated]

OLD TESTAMENT

The Lord our God says to his people: 'Listen! Listen to ME. Listen MY people (Psalm 81:8&13). Be silent before ME (Isaiah 41:1, NIV). Be still (Psalm 46:10, BCP). Be attentive to every word of MINE (Exodus 23:13). It is to you I call, MY people who know what is right (Proverbs 8:3), you who lay MY law to heart (Isaiah 51:7). Draw near to ME (Isaiah 48:16). Listen carefully to all that I have to say to you, and take it to heart (Ezekiel 3:10). I will speak clearly, you will have plain speech from ME. I speak nothing but truth. All that I say is right, all is straightforward (Proverbs 8:6–8). I declare what is just (Isaiah 45:19). Listen to instruction and grow wise (Proverbs 8:33). Listen carefully to ME and eat what is good (Isaiah 55:2, NRSV). Hold fast to my words with all your heart, keep my commandments, and you will have life (Proverbs 4:4) The person I look to is one who reveres MY words (Isaiah 66:2, NEB). I put MY words in your mouth (Isaiah 51:16). Are not my words like fire, says the Lord; are they not like a hammer that shatters rock? (Jeremiah 23:29). You must listen to what I say (Proverbs 7:24). You must speak MY words (Ezekiel 2:7). I will give you the power of speech (Ezekiel 3:27). I, the Lord, will say what I will, and it shall be done (Ezekiel 12:25); I will speak, I will act (Ezekiel 22:14). No words of MINE shall be delayed; even as I speak, it shall be done (Ezekiel 12:28, NEB). Go, tell everything (Jeremiah 1:17), declare and proclaim among the nations (Joel 3:9), spread the news, keep nothing back (Jeremiah 50:2). MY words which I put into your mouth will never fail you; (Isaiah 59:21). As the rain and the snow come down from heaven and do not return until they have watered the earth, so shall the word which comes forth from MY mouth prevail; it shall not return to ME fruitless, without accomplishing MY purpose' (Isaiah 55:10).

NEW TESTAMENT

Our Lord Jesus Christ says to his people: 'Listen to ME and understand (Mark 7:14). To you who are MY friends I say, "Do not fear" (Luke 12:4). Be still (Mark 4:39), be silent (Mark 1:25), be opened (Mark 7:34). Take note of what you hear (Mark 4:24). What I say is for you (Mark 13:37). Take care how you listen (Luke 8:18). MY task is to bear witness to the truth, and all who are not deaf to truth listen to MY voice (John 18:37). Anyone who loves ME will heed what I say (John 14:23). The words I speak to you are both spirit and life (John 6:63). MY words will never pass away (Mark 13:31). What I say to you, I say to everyone (Mark 13:37). What I say to you, you must repeat. What you hear, you must shout from the housetops (Matthew 10:27). Go and tell everything God has done for you (Luke 8:39). You must go and announce the kingdom of God (Luke 9:60). Go and proclaim the Good News to the whole creation (Mark 16:15). The words you need will be given you (Matthew 10:19). I MYSELF will give you power of utterance (Luke 21:15, NEB). Say whatever is given you to say; for it is not you who will be speaking, but the Holy Spirit' (Mark 13:11).

These sequences of sayings from the two testaments are the fruit of many hours labour. The selection was made with great care to avoid, as far as possible, any out-of-context distortion of their original meaning. The same principle applies to the use of scripture throughout this book.

3 David E. Rosage, *Listen to Him – A Daily guide to Scriptural Prayer* (Servant Publications, 1981), p.40.
4 Psalms 42:1–2; 46:10; 62:1; 63:1–2; 108:1.
5 Matthew 4:1–11. Desert experience is a common feature of the mystical/contemplative tradition. See, among other writings, the following:

Helen Waddell
The Desert Fathers (Constable)

Thomas Merton
The Wisdom of the Desert (Sheldon Press, 1973)

Carlo Carretto
The Desert in the City (Collins, 1979)

Henri Nouwen
The Way of the Desert – Desert Spirituality and Contemporary Ministry (DLT, 1981)

Catherine de Hueck Doherty
Poustinia (Fount,1977)

Kenneth Leech
True God (SPCK, 1985), Chapter 5.

Alan Jones
Soul Making – The Desert Way of Spirituality (SCM Press, 1986)

Here is a brief quotation from the last of these (p.6):

The desert is 'the arena . . . especially chosen by God as the focus of his revelation. Thus the desert of which I speak is a desert of the spirit: a place of silence, waiting and temptation. It is also a place of revelation, conversion, and transformation. A true revelation is a very disturbing event because it demands a response; and to respond to it means some kind of inner revolution. It involves being . . . made new, being "born again". The desert, then, is a place of revelation and revolution. In the desert we wait, we weep, we learn to live.'

6 See also Thomas Merton's *Seeds of Contemplation* (Anthony Clarke Books, 1972), Chapter 3.

7 The Word of God is also, for example: milk, honey, good food (1 Peter 2:2; Ezekiel 3:3; Isaiah 55:2); a light (Psalm 119:105); hammer, nails, goad (Jeremiah 23:30; Ecclesiastes 11:11); pure silver and gold (Psalm 12:6); truth (1 Kings 17:24; Psalm 119:160; Proverbs 8:6; Daniel 11:2; John 1:14; 17:17; 18:37); life, eternal life, alive, living (Psalm 119:25; John 5:24; 6:63; 6:68; Hebrews 4:12; 1 Peter 1:23; 1 John 1:2); active, piercing, sifting, exposing, cleansing (Ezekiel 22:15; 37:14; Hebrews 4:12–13; John 15:3); flesh (John 1:14); Spirit/spirit (Mathew 10:20; John 6:63); indwelling (John 15:7); God (John 1:1); a thrill in the heart (Psalm 119:161).

Chapter 4

1 Article 'Fasting' in Gordon Wakefield's *A Dictionary of Christian Spirituality* (SCM Press, 1983).

2 Try Shirley Ross, *Fasting* (Sheldon Press, 1973); Thomas Ryan, *Fasting Rediscovered* (Paulist Press, 1981); Richard Foster, *Celebration of Discipline* (revised edition; Hodder & Stoughton, 1989) Part 1, Chapter 4.

3 Patrick Woodhouse, *Beyond Words* (Kevin Mayhew, 2001).

4 The Reverend Dr Martin Israel, a distinguished pathologist, former lecturer at the Royal College of Surgeons, and a priest in the Church of England, has been described as

'one of the most sought after spiritual guides in this country'. He is deeply involved in healing, counselling and spiritual direction.

Chapter 5

1 The leader at a retreat is often known as a *conductor*. Robert Coulson preferred not to use this word. Instead, he coined the phrase *Witness of the Word of God* for anyone who was 'leading' a contemplative exercise, whether at a retreat, a quiet day, or a prayer group. This is often shortened to *Witness of the Word*, or simply *Witness*.

2 A good general book on the subject is Herbert Benson's *The Relaxation Response* (Collins/Fountain, 1977). Chapter 5 is particularly relevant to the contemplative.

3 cf. Augustine of Hippo, *Confessions* (e.g. edition from Labarum Publications, 1986), Book One, in which he expresses to God his great religious discovery: 'You have made us to be "toward" you, and our heart is restless until it rests in you.'

Chapter 6

1 A classic account is St Athanasius's *The Life of Anthony* (SPCK, 1980). St Anthony of Egypt, endeavouring to 'pray without ceasing', experienced many temptations in his quest for perfection. Athanasius describes the terrible conflict of Anthony's 'spiritual warfare'. Another classic treatment is Lorenzo Scupoli's *The Spiritual Combat* (Anthony Clarke Books), in which he speaks of waging 'a constant, cruel war with yourself'. But see also Robert Llewelyn's *The Positive Role of Distraction in Prayer* (SLG Press, 1977).

2 Exodus 20:24; Genesis 26:3; Isaiah 41:10; John 15:16; Ezekiel 22:15; Jeremiah 31:3; 2 Samuel 7:15; Jeremiah 14:17; Isaiah 42:1; Matthew 11:28; Jeremiah 3:14; John 14:1; Deuteronomy 30:19–20; Genesis 17:2, 26:24, 3:9; 1 Kings 19:9; Matthew 9:28. These represent *some* of the categories. Some sayings occur time and time again, in

one form or another, throughout the Scriptures: e.g. 'Do not be afraid, for I AM with you.'

Everything that God is represented as saying is addressed either to a nation or to individual people. You may often find it helpful to interpolate your own name. This is a reminder that God is speaking to you personally. You need to hear and receive the Word within yourself before you can speak it out, *in his Name*, to others in intercession.

Chapter 7

1 David Torkington, *The Prophet: The Inner Meaning of Prayer* (Spennithorne Publications, 1987).
2 See Chapter 5, the section entitled *The Invitation*.
3 A prayer of thanksgiving and rededication may be cast in any form of words. The prayer most frequently used in the Fellowship of Contemplative Prayer is one that the founder himself composed and used:

> *Father, we thank you for all your unsearchable riches, which pour forth from you as light pours from the sun, in boundless profusion and generosity, whether received, ignored, or rejected. And now (once again) we offer to you, in so far as we are able, as an emptiness to be filled with your divine fullness, ourselves – our souls and bodies – all that we have, all that we are, and all that we do, a living sacrifice.*

Another good prayer is the Prayer of Dedication sometimes used at the end of a church service:

> *Almighty God, we thank you for the gift of your holy word. May it be a lantern to our feet, a light to our paths, and a strength to our lives. Take us and use us to love and serve others, in the power of the Holy Spirit, and in the name of your Son, Jesus Christ our Lord. Amen.*

Or for a simple, direct, and biblical prayer, use the response of Mary to the angel's message:

> 'Let it be to me [us] according to your Word.'

Chapter 9

1 If you are interested to know the full story, you can read about it in the biography of Robert Coulson by Martin Tunnicliffe entitled *Spirit and Life*. This was published in 1988 and is now out of print, but a loan copy is available either from a Fellowship member who owns one, or from the author by writing to 202 Ralph Road, Solihull, West Midlands B90 3LE enclosing stamps for postage costs.

Chapter 10

1 Psalms 26:8; 93:5; 65:4; 5:7–8; 66:13; 36:8; 84:3–4; 48:9–10.
2 Cf. Songs of Songs 8:6–7; Hosea 11:8; Exodus 22–27; Jeremiah 31:20.
3 Quoted in Whitall N. Perry *A Treasury of Traditional Wisdom* (Perennial Books, 1971), p.311.